Grace & Peace

A Plea for Spiritual Humility

J.K. Hodge

Printed in the United States of America

First Printing, 2014

ISBN-10 069-223-976-6
ISBN-13 978-0-6922397-6-6

Zeteo

PRESS

Hudsonville, MI 49426
info@zeteopress.com

Contents

Prologue

One morning, about ten years ago, my friend Paulo and I sat down at Cracker Barrel to enjoy one last meal together. For several years, we had met for our weekly breakfasts, but this time was different. Later that day, Paulo and his wife would board a plane to Kuwait City to begin a new life teaching abroad. I was excited for Paulo, but I knew also that I would miss him a great deal.

Goodbyes are never easy. In this case, however, the relative finality of the meal we shared led to one of the most honest and authentic conversations about faith that either of us had ever experienced. To this day, I view that conversation as a turning point in my spiritual journey.

I don't remember all of the details, but what I do remember is that each of us shared perspectives on life, God, and the church that we had thought about for a long time, but had never dared to say out loud.

Both of us had become disillusioned by the conservative Christian subculture that surrounded us. We had each experienced pride, hypocrisy, and divisiveness within the body of Christ. Paulo had borne the brunt of it as a worship leader on the staff of two different churches, but my experiences in other settings mirrored his. It was refreshing to both of us to know that we were not the only ones to feel the way we did. By the end of our long breakfast, we had each come to realize that there were very few other people in our lives with whom we could have had such an honest conversation.

Several years later, I found myself at a different table, sharing a meal with an avowed atheist I'll call Tom. I had met Tom only recently, and I knew very little about him. Our conversation that night was sparked by the invocation that was given prior to the banquet we were attending. After the prayer, Tom mentioned something about how people could believe in superstitions if they wanted to, but he didn't want anything to do with it.

It was a harsh comment, and it would have been easy for me to be offended. I was tempted to just ignore what Tom had said and go back to eating my salad, but for some reason, I decided to try to learn a bit more about his point of view.

As it turns out, what bothered Tom the most was the fact that a Christian invocation had been given at a conference that was, ironically, focused on diversity. I could agree with Tom on that. As a Christian, I had found the prayer to be out of place, particularly since the conference participants included members of many different faiths, and some who, like Tom, did not consider themselves to be a part of any faith. I shared my thoughts with Tom, and we ended up talking for probably 20 or 30 minutes.

I learned a lot from that conversation. For instance, I discovered that Tom thought quite highly of Jesus. Unfortunately, he had seen very little of Jesus in the Christian communities he had encountered throughout his life. Instead, he had observed from the outside what my friend Paulo and I had experienced from within. To Tom, modern-day Christianity seemed far removed from—and even antithetical to—the teachings of Christ. I couldn't have agreed more.

We had a great discussion, and I think it's safe to say that both of us were surprised by the extent to which we found ourselves agreeing with each other. In spite of significant differences in our religious beliefs and backgrounds, our experiences of the church had been remarkably similar. Interestingly, our conversation ended on the same note as my breakfast with Paulo nearly a decade earlier. We left the banquet thanking each other for the conversation and acknowledging that there were very few other people with whom we could have had such a constructive and enlightening dialogue about our religious views and experiences.

I share these stories because they serve to illustrate a few of the observations that led me to write this book.

First, folks both within and outside of Christianity have experienced attitudes and behaviors from professing Christians that stand in stark contrast to the teachings of Jesus.

Second, open and honest dialogue about religious differences seems to be the exception rather than the rule. Discussion of religion is perceived by many to be an inherently risky activity—one to be avoided or, at the very least, approached with extreme caution.

Finally, people are often not as different as they may seem at first glance. There is a lot to be said for taking the time to understand a perspective that differs from one's own. Defensiveness, insecurity, and fear may inhibit us from doing so, but it need not be this way.

This book is my way of extending my conversations with Paulo and Tom—and many others—to a broader context.

To those within the church, I hope that you can relate to at least some of what I am about to say.

To those outside the church, I hope that my perspectives provide some balance to what you may have encountered in the past.

And to all who take the time to read these words, thank you. I hope you will find that, whatever doubts, concerns, or frustrations you may have about Christians and Christianity, you are not alone.

Part I

The Problem of Pride

Chapter 1

Pride

"Grace and peace be with you."

To those who follow Jesus Christ, these are beautiful and familiar words. Christians believe in a God of grace, a God of peace. And so we wish each other grace, and we wish each other peace. But these words ought to be more than just a friendly pleasantry. At their core, they are an exhortation, a challenge to live lives that reflect the God we profess.

Are we living up to this challenge? In our daily lives, do our words and our deeds, our attitudes and our behaviors—particularly toward those who act or believe differently than we do—extend grace and promote peace? If one were to paint a picture of our God based solely on what they observed in us, would that picture look anything like the one we paint on Sunday mornings through our songs, our liturgies, and our three-point sermons? Would it bear any resemblance to the God of whom scripture testifies?

"The Lord is gracious and compassionate, slow to anger and rich in love."[1] Are we?

"Blessed are the peacemakers, for they will be called children of God."[2] Are we living out our calling as daughters and sons of the God of peace?

Too often, the answer to these questions is no. The wars of modern-day Christianity are fought through billboards, picket signs, boycotts, blog posts, and hastily-sent tweets. They may be less bloody than the crusades of the past, but the wounds they inflict are severe nonetheless.

These charges deserve an explanation, and I will give one. But first, let me simply acknowledge that I share in the blame for this predicament. I am an aspiring but imperfect Christ-follower, and I have often failed to follow my own advice. Insofar as I have contributed to the problem that I am trying to solve, I am a party to any indictment I can put forth. And so it is in that spirit—not as an outsider looking in, but as one who belongs to the body of Christ and shares responsibility for her shortcomings—that I offer these words.

So what exactly is the problem, and where have we gone astray?

---

[1] Psalm 145:8
[2] Matthew 5:9

In my view, we as Christians have succumbed to what C.S. Lewis called "the great sin": pride. The dictionary defines pride to be "the quality of having an excessively high opinion of oneself or one's importance."[3] Within today's American Christian subculture, pride is endemic.

The kind of pride that I am talking about begins with the life of the mind—in particular, an overinflated and unrealistic view of humanity's ability to make sense of the divine and find answers to life's most difficult questions. It evolves to fear-based authoritarianism, which in turn leads to a faith that is narrow, self-focused, and exclusive.

We are called to trust in the Lord, to seek truth, and to love our neighbor.

Instead, we trust in our own understanding, we seek security through certainty, and we love only those "neighbors" who share our beliefs and values.

We have become gods unto ourselves, worshiping at the altar of knowledge and reason.

We conflate truth and opinion, blind to our self-serving biases and oblivious to the limitations of our human intellect. We exalt our interpretation of the truth as *the*

---

[3] *New Oxford American Dictionary*. Retrieved from http://www.oxforddictionaries.com/us/definition/american_english/pride

truth, castigating and ostracizing those who view the world through different lenses.

We worship the Bible, and our understanding of it, rather than the One to whom it points.

We idolize certainty and vilify doubt. Questions are viewed as threats, as are those who pose questions.

Our security rests in our being right, and so we spend countless hours debating doctrine and taking positions on issues that are beyond our comprehension—issues that, truth be told, should have little to no bearing on the way we live out our faith.

Rather than loving our neighbors and uniting under the banner of Christ, we draw divisions based on belief. We oversimplify positions, exaggerate differences, and insist on divisive either/or thinking. Those who believe differently become targets of persuasion rather than love.

We are, in short, a prideful people, and the consequences are devastating.

As I write these strong words, I am aware that I am painting with a rather broad brush. I do not mean to suggest that all Christians are prideful, or that Christians are incapable of grace, peace, love, and humility. This is certainly not the case. But pride is a disease that, if left unchecked, will destroy the entire body. Moreover, the problem of pride is pervasive enough that no follower of Christ should believe for a moment that they are immune to it.

In 2007, the Barna group published extensive research on how young people unaffiliated with the church perceive Christians and Christianity. The results were not encouraging. In particular, their study revealed that the vast majority of outsiders view Christians as hypocritical, disingenuous, agenda-driven (particularly with regard to evangelism), bigoted, sheltered, overly political, and judgmental—traits that I would argue all have their roots in spiritual pride. [4]

Of course, one could claim that these perceptions are inaccurate, or that, as Paul writes, "the message of the cross is foolishness to those who are perishing, but to us who are being saved it is the power of God." [5] Perhaps the perceptions of outsiders are simply a fulfillment of Jesus' words that followers of Christ "will be hated by everyone because of me." [6] This could indeed be the case. Or it could be nothing more than a convenient rationalization.

---

[4] Kinnaman, D., & Lyons, G. (2007). *Unchristian: What a new generation really thinks about Christianity… and why it matters.* Grand Rapids, MI: Baker Books. (pp. 29-30)

[5] 1 Corinthians 1:18

[6] Matthew 10:22; see also Luke 21:17, Mark 13:13.

It is easy for those outside of the church to criticize her weaknesses. It is also easy for those within the church to simply dismiss this criticism as uninformed or not representative of the church as a whole. This, however, is a dangerous path to tread.

Regardless of whether one agrees with the perceptions of those outside the church, to simply ignore them is not only self-serving but ultimately counterproductive to the cause of Christ. Perceptions matter. In fact, they are sometimes *all* that matters. As social conflict researchers Pruitt and Kim observe, "perceptions ordinarily have an immediate impact on behavior... whereas reality works more slowly and with less certainty."[7] If the way we practice our faith serves to alienate the very people we aim to reach, then how are we living out our calling to "go and make disciples of all nations"?[8]

Speaking of discipleship, Jesus said that his disciples would be known by their love for each other.[9] But even (and perhaps especially) *within* the church, we fall short of the apostle Paul's exhortation to "be completely humble and gentle," to "be patient, bearing with one another in

---

[7] Pruitt, D. G., & Kim, S. H. (2004). *Social conflict: Escalation, stalemate, and settlement* (3rd ed.). New York, NY: McGraw-Hill. (p. 8)
[8] Matthew 28:19
[9] John 13:35

love," and to "make every effort to keep the unity of the Spirit through the bond of peace."[10]

Something is not right. All is not well within the body of Christ. And, frankly, I think that we are sometimes afraid (or ashamed) to admit the sorry state of affairs we find ourselves in.

It can indeed be difficult to acknowledge that the church, referred to in scripture as the bride of Christ, is flawed. In fact, one could argue that to love Christ is to love the church. But loving something—or someone—does not entail turning a blind eye to its failures.

I love my wife deeply. Apart from life itself, she is unquestionably the greatest earthly blessing that God has ever seen fit to bestow upon me. But my wife is not perfect, and my marriage would be a sham if I were not willing to admit that. Indeed, a good marriage—really, any healthy relationship—serves to help both partners grow and improve themselves over time.

This is why, in the movie *As Good as It Gets*, when Jack Nicholson's character tells his love interest (played by Helen Hunt), "You make me want to be a better man," she responds, "That's maybe the best compliment of my life."

---

[10] Ephesians 4:2-3

And so it is with the church. It is not a betrayal, but rather an act of love, to acknowledge—with humility and a longing for redemption—the shortcomings in Christ's bride and her current state in this fallen world. In fact, as Christians, it is our calling to help prepare the bride of Christ for the great wedding feast that is yet to come on the day when all things will be made new.

I believe that spiritual pride is keeping the church from being all that God intends her to be. And so this book is a plea to my fellow brothers and sisters in Christ to live out a more humble and gentle faith—one that does not, as my friend Rick Hopkins so eloquently puts it, fight for its rightness at the cost of its purpose.

Before we move on, a few clarifications are in order.

First, this book is not a *case*, but rather a *plea*. The dictionary defines the former to be "a set of facts or arguments supporting one side of a debate or controversy," whereas the latter is "a request made in an urgent and emotional manner."[11]

This distinction is important because it is not my intention to attempt to convince you that spiritual pride *is* in fact a problem within the church. In the past few pages, I have

---

[11] *New Oxford American Dictionary*. Retrieved from
http://www.oxforddictionaries.com/us/definition/american_english/case;
http://www.oxforddictionaries.com/us/definition/american_english/plea

shared with you my convictions about the problem of pride—convictions that I believe the Holy Spirit has laid on my heart over the course of much of my adult life. If you do not share these convictions to some extent—that is, if the words I have written so far do not resonate with you in some way—then it is not my primary goal to try to convince you otherwise. Of course, I welcome you to read on, but I will not be surprised or offended if, at the end of the day, you remain skeptical of what I have to say.

This book is really intended for those who love the church but know in their hearts that something needs to change. It is for those who have experienced or perpetrated spiritual pride but may not have recognized it as such. It is for those who long to ask hard questions but have been led to believe that doing so is tantamount to spiritual treason. It is for those who seek to better understand the problem of pride so that they can be a part of the solution. And, perhaps most importantly, it is for those have the courage to peer into the dark corners of their psyches and come face to face with the brokenness that lies within.

Because it is there that healing begins. If pride is the quality of having an excessively high opinion of oneself or one's importance, then humility can be thought of as having a proper view of oneself in relation to God and others. To cultivate such a view, we must first come to understand, acknowledge, and live within the context of our many weaknesses and limitations. And so that is where our journey will start.

The first half of this book attempts to elucidate the root causes and manifestations of spiritual pride. To do so, it draws on perspectives from psychology, sociology, and even mathematics. The second half of the book is a series of four reflections on the practice of spiritual humility.

In the interest of full disclosure, you should know that I am neither a theologian nor a bible scholar. My background is in academia, where I am a professor and administrator at a large, state university. I hold graduate degrees in mathematics and in conflict resolution, and much of what I have written here is based on research in the psychology and sociology of religion. However, my thinking on broader spiritual matters has emerged not from any kind of formal educational training, but rather from my own walk with God and my interactions with others who seek to know Him. Therefore, when I quote biblical passages, my intent is not to establish a comprehensive theological basis for my ideas, but rather to express beliefs, viewpoints, and perspectives using the language of scripture. I don't think that anything I have written here is unbiblical or inconsistent with the overarching narrative of scripture. With that said, I have neither the expertise nor the desire to use the Bible as a tool to "prove" my positions. In fact, to do so would be self-defeating and contradictory to my message, as you will see in the pages to come.

I hope that as you read these words, you will feel free to question, challenge, or disagree with my perspectives. I don't claim that my views, experiences, or interpretation of scripture are authoritative in any way. I am but one voice among many, and so I encourage you to read this book with a prayerful heart and a discerning mind.

There are two sayings of Jesus that have helped me in this regard, and I would like to share them with you before we move on.

The first is from the gospel of John, where Jesus tells his disciples that "when he, the Spirit of truth, comes, he will guide you into all the truth."[12] I keep this verse in a frame on my desk to remind myself of the importance of the Holy Spirit in my quest to know God and His truth.

The second is from Luke, where Jesus makes the simple but profound observation that "wisdom is shown to be right by the lives of those who follow it."[13] As I have encountered various moral, political, and theological perspectives over the years, this verse has provided a

---

[12] John 16:13
[13] Luke 7:35 (NLT)

great deal of clarity. I hope that it does the same for you as we delve into the problem of pride.

Chapter 2

Reason

I used to love a good theological debate.

When I was an undergraduate at Calvin College, I belonged to a group of 12 students—three from each class—called the *Men of the Institutes*. Every Tuesday night, we would retreat to the basement of a little house on campus to diligently study the words of John Calvin's *Institutes of the Christian Religion*.[14]

Originally published in Latin in 1536, the *Institutes* are a collection of four books which, depending on the translation, amount to somewhere around 1200 pages of not-so-light reading.

In the preface to the 1545 French edition, Calvin explains his goal in writing the *Institutes* as follows:

> Although the Holy Scriptures contain a perfect doctrine, to which nothing can be added—our Lord having been pleased therein to unfold the infinite treasures

---

[14] Calvin's Institutes are widely available online; see, for example, http://www.ccel.org/ccel/calvin/institutes/

of his wisdom—still every person, not intimately acquainted with them, stands in need of some guidance and direction, as to what he ought to look for in them, that he may not wander up and down, but pursue a certain path, and so attain the end to which the Holy Spirit invites him.

Hence it is the duty of those who have received from God more light than others to assist the simple in this matter, and, as it were, lend them their hand to guide and assist them in finding the sum of what God has been pleased to teach us in his word. Now, this cannot be better done in writing than by treating in succession of the principal matters which are comprised in Christian philosophy. For he who understands these will be prepared to make more progress in the school of God in one day than any other person in three months, inasmuch as he, in a great measure, knows to what he should refer each sentence, and has a rule by which to test whatever is presented to him.

Seeing, then, how necessary it was in this manner to aid those who desire to be instructed in the doctrine of salvation, I have endeavoured, according to the ability which God has given me, to employ myself in so doing, and with this view have composed the present book.

John Calvin was one of the most influential voices in reformation theology, and to this day his contributions have left a lasting impact on the church. John Calvin was also a man who was confident in his abilities to understand the things of God—to make perfect sense of the "perfect doctrine" contained in scripture. He believed that he had "received from God more light than others" and that it was his "duty" to "assist the simple" in "finding the sum of what God has been pleased to teach us in his word."

Nearly 500 years later, this same spirit is alive and well within the church. A walk through the aisles of any Christian bookstore will quickly reveal that there is no shortage of authors who view it as their duty to illuminate for the rest of us the truths of scripture that God has revealed to them. They promise to make the Bible "plain, simple, and understandable." They reveal "God's simple truth" about marriage, finances, proper dietary habits, and the second coming of Christ. They present "five simple steps" to a spirit-filled life. And they even suggest that following Jesus can be "made simple."

Underlying this approach is a belief that, on virtually every topic pertaining to the spiritual life, there is one indisputable truth revealed in scripture, and this truth is accessible to those who properly apply their powers of intellect and reason.

In many ways, this perspective is appealing. We like to think of ourselves as rational and able to make sense of the world around us, even though our life experiences often bring more questions than answers. Still, we do our best to try to make it all add up to something coherent and at least somewhat palatable, never quite arriving at our final destination but believing all the while that perhaps someday we will.

The problem is that we are not as rational as we like to think we are. We are not objective observers of the world around us, and more often than not we use logic and reason not to arrive at unbiased conclusions from neutral assumptions, but rather to construct arguments to support the views we already hold.

A study by marketing professor Raj Raghunathan and Ph.D. student Szu-Chi Huang[15] provides a good illustration of this phenomenon, which is known as *post-hoc rationalization*. In part of the study, participants were shown pictures of two chickens. One looked healthy and plump while the other looked thin and sickly. Half of the participants were told that the plump chicken was healthier but less tasty, while the other half was told the same about the thin chicken.

Not surprisingly, both groups overwhelmingly said that they preferred the plump chicken, but for different reasons. Those who had been told that the plump chicken was healthier but less tasty said that they valued health above taste. Those who had been told the opposite said that they valued taste above health. In other words, both groups came to the same decision, but used a different

---

[15] Rich, H. (April 23, 2010). Do you make buying decisions based on logic or emotion? A tale of two chickens. Retrieved from bit.ly/1608VlY

rationale—based on the information that was available to them—to justify it.

The reason is simple: people don't like the thought of eating sickly-looking chickens, even if they are told that such chickens are healthier (or tastier) than other more visually appealing alternatives. At the same time, most people realize that it is irrational to say that health is more important than taste and then still choose the chicken that is reportedly less healthy.

Simply put, we want to choose the good-looking chicken. We also want to think of ourselves as rational. And so we find a justification to support the decision we want to make, even if doing so involves augmenting, misrepresenting, or flat-out lying about our values in order to provide support for our emotional inclinations.

Raghunathan summarizes the problem as follows:

> In our society it is generally not considered justifiable to make a decision purely on an emotional response. ... We want to be considered scientific and rational, so we come up with reasons after the fact to justify our choice.
>
> This process seems to be happening somewhat unconsciously, people are not really aware they're coming up with these justifications. What is even more interesting is that people who claim that emotions are not that important, who consider themselves to be really rational, are actually more prone to fall into this trap.

Intriguing, no? And that's just the beginning. Psychologists have documented a multitude of other ways in which humans exhibit bias in their cognitive processes.

Take, for example, confirmation bias, which is closely related to post-hoc rationalization. Rather than objectively processing all available information to come to an informed conclusion, we actually tend to seek out information that supports our already-formed positions and ignore perspectives that may pose a challenge to these positions. Negotiation experts Fisher, Ury, and Patton put it this way in their landmark book *Getting to Yes*:

> How you see the world depends on where you sit. People tend to see what they want to see. Out of a mass of detailed information, they tend to pick out and focus on those facts that confirm their prior perceptions and to disregard or misinterpret those that call their perceptions into question.[16]

Consider, for instance, the last time you sought advice on an important decision. Chances are you already had some idea of what you wanted to do and were looking for some kind of confirmation. Did you seek the opinion of someone you suspected would be supportive, or did you actively solicit input from those who you knew would be

---

[16] Fisher, R., Ury, W., & Patton, B. (1991). *Getting to yes: Negotiating agreement without giving in.* 2nd ed. New York, NY: Penguin Books. (p. 23)

skeptical of your decision? Most of us do the former; if we are wise enough to seek feedback from both supporters and critics, then we have taken the first steps toward overcoming confirmation bias, and our decisions will likely be better and more informed because of this.

But even if we are able to seek out information in a reasonably objective manner, we still face the problem of selective interpretation. Whether we are aware of it or not, each of us views the world through our own unique lens of interpretation that is shaped by our upbringing, our education, our culture, our experiences, and our interactions with others. This is why two people can view the exact same information and come to vastly different conclusions.

Interpretive bias poses a particular challenge to the way many Christians approach scripture. According to Notre Dame sociologist Christian Smith, the widely-held *biblicist* approach insists that the Bible is clear, self-contained, and internally consistent; that "any reasonably intelligent person can read the Bible in his or her own language and correctly understand the plain meaning of the text"; and that "all matters of Christian belief and practice can be learned by sitting down with the Bible and piecing together the clear 'biblical' truths that it teaches."[17]

The problem with the biblicist approach is what Smith refers to as *pervasive interpretive pluralism*, described as follows:

> … on important matters the Bible apparently is not clear, consistent, and univocal enough to enable the best-intentioned, most highly skilled, believing readers to come to agreement as to what it teaches. That is an empirical, historical, undeniable, and ever-present reality. [18]

Smith goes on to pose an important question:

> … if the Bible is given by a truthful and omnipotent God as an internally consistent and perspicuous text precisely for the purpose of revealing to humans correct beliefs, practices, and morals, then *why is it that the presumably sincere Christians to whom it has been given cannot read it and come to common agreement about what it teaches?*[19]

What if Christians cannot agree on even basic doctrinal issues because no two Christians view the Bible through the same lens? What if, in presenting ourselves as objective seekers of the truth and insisting that our view of

---

[17] Smith, C. (2011). *The Bible made impossible: Why biblicism is not a truly evangelical reading of scripture.* Grand Rapids, MI: Brazos Press. (pp. 4-5)
[18] Ibid., p. 25.
[19] Ibid., p. 26.

scripture is the "right" view, we have overlooked the fact that our cognitive biases make the very notion of objectivity impossible? Is it not ironic that so many Christians, who are quick to profess that all of humanity is fallen and in need of redemption, seem alarmingly content to accept without hesitation the power of the human mind to make sense of the things of God? This is simply an untenable position, and one that reeks of pride.

But let's put aside these objections for the time being and assume the existence of an individual so pure and so self-aware as to avoid the self-serving biases that plague the rest of humanity. Would such an individual be able to construct a completely accurate and coherent picture of God?

To gain insight into this question, we'll turn to—perhaps surprisingly—mathematics. I am going to keep the discussion fairly brief here (an act of mercy for those readers who are less mathematically inclined), but if you'd like to know more, there is an appendix at the end of the chapter that provides some additional details.

I mentioned earlier that I used to like a good theological debate. Truth be told, I think the mathematician in me still does. You see, mathematicians prove things. We start with self-evident assumptions, called *axioms*, and we then apply logic and reason to arrive at indisputable conclusions. The process is not all that different from the way many Christians approach theology.

As a mathematician, I have a lot of faith in the power of reason. But mathematicians realized nearly 100 years ago that even reason has its limitations. In 1931, Austrian mathematician Kurt Gödel proved that any axiom system that is both consistent (incapable of yielding contradictory results) and robust enough to allow for basic arithmetic cannot possibly be complete—that is, there are statements that are verifiably true but cannot be proved from the axioms.

What does this have to do with spiritual humility?

First, we all have axioms. No matter how logical or objective we think we are, there are certain truths that we hold to be self-evident and that, for lack of a better term, we take on faith. To find out what your axioms are, think of any belief that is personally significant to you and that you hold with a high degree of conviction. Then ask yourself, "Why do I believe this?" For each reason you are able to come up with, ask yourself, "Why do I believe *that*?" If you repeat this process for long enough, you will eventually come to a point where you have exhausted your ability to rationally justify your beliefs. In doing so, you will have discovered your axioms: the basic starting points that form the core of your belief system.

Second, even our most foundational beliefs—our axioms, if you will—are not static. They often change—or, I would argue, *should* change—as we encounter God in new ways and experience both the trials and triumphs of life. Sometimes these changes are dramatic, leading us to views that differ greatly from those we held in the past. In other cases, the primary content of our beliefs may remain the same even as the way we hold these beliefs evolves to reflect a more nuanced, complex, and multi-layered understanding of God and the world around us.

And, of course, all but the most die-hard relativists will admit that it is possible to hold views that are simply at odds with reality. Our relative confidence in the correctness of our beliefs belies the seriousness of this problem.

In order to navigate life, we constantly make assumptions—often at a subconscious level—that help us make sense of the world around us. These assumptions influence the decisions we make, how we interpret events that we experience, and even our most deeply held beliefs. This, of course, begs the question: What are the chances that *all* of our assumptions are correct? As any mathematician knows, the conclusions we draw are only as good as the assumptions we begin with. If one assumption turns out to be false, then the whole argument

can fall apart. How confident can we be that our axioms—
all of them—are accurate and reliable starting points?

Finally—and this is what brings us back to Gödel—
whatever axioms we begin with, we would be wise to
proceed with a healthy degree of skepticism about what
we can and cannot know as a consequence of these
axioms. Logic and reason have limited reach—even, as
Gödel showed, in the context of basic arithmetic. It is
important to note here that I am not talking about our
abilities to apply logic properly (although, as we discussed
earlier, this is a cause for concern). Rather, I am suggesting
that logic itself has inherent limitations and that we are
foolish to act as if it does not, particularly when applied to
the divine.

It would not be good mathematics to generalize Gödel's
work too far beyond its original scope. So let me be clear:
Gödel's incompleteness theorem does not *prove* that our
abilities to reason about God are flawed. But it does
provide a perspective that can shed light on some of the
difficulties we face in this regard.

As mathematicians James Bradley and Russell Howell
suggest:

> ... perhaps Gödel's incompleteness theorem applies in
> some way to all areas that operate with a certain core of
> logical substrata. In the working out of our world and life
> view, of course we strive for both consistency and

completeness. However, as we near one of these ideals, it appears at times to be the opposite of the other. Does our Christian world and life view appear paradoxical? Perhaps it is because it needs reworking, and because it is somewhat inconsistent. Perhaps, on the other hand, we see paradoxical things in the scriptures precisely because they give us a fairly *complete* picture of God. Perhaps to our finite and fallen minds a complete picture of God appears somewhat inconsistent. [20]

Bradley and Howell argue that the tension between consistency and completeness ought to lead to "a certain amount of epistemological humility in dialoguing with others," and that "although we strive for both consistency and completeness, if we take an honest look at where we are at any moment, we'll probably admit that we don't have either." [21]

That last line bears repeating: If we are honest (and this is a big if), we'll probably admit that our views about God are neither complete nor consistent.

The problem is that most Christians are not even aware of the tension between consistency and completeness and therefore have given very little thought to its implications—which, for endeavors such as biblical

---

[20] Bradley, W. J., and Howell, R. (2001). *Mathematics in a postmodern age: A Christian perspective.* Grand Rapids, MI: Eerdmans Publishing Co. (p. 383)

[21] Ibid., p. 384.

interpretation, are significant. Christian Smith provides this
analogy:

> Consider… [that] the Bible functions something
> like… an enormous jigsaw puzzle with a huge number of
> pieces that is sold in many stores. The job of the Bible
> interpreter in this analogy is to figure out how the scads of
> pieces dumped from the box and spread all over a table fit
> together to make the finished puzzle picture. The only
> difficulty is that this is a very unusual puzzle. For, as far as
> anyone working on it can figure out, different puzzle pieces
> can fit together in different ways to make distinctly
> different portraits. …
>
> Not only that, but in any given picture, enough of the
> pieces fit together to fill in most of the image, but not all
> of it. Every picture, no matter how well it is put together,
> still has some missing puzzle pieces. … Furthermore, no
> matter how the pieces are fit together to make a nearly
> finished picture, there are always some pieces that do not
> fit. In no picture do *all* the pieces correctly fit together.
> Some people try, but they end up bending and mangling
> those pieces. It just doesn't work. [22]

Are our efforts to make sense of God ultimately a fool's
errand? Are we trying too hard to piece together a puzzle
that has no hope of being assembled with the tools we
have at our disposal?

---

[22] Ibid., pp. 45-46.

One of the most familiar commands in scripture is found in the book of Proverbs: "Trust in the LORD with all your heart and lean not on your own understanding."[23] What if this command, like so many others, is not meant to restrict us, but rather to free us from the limitations of our intellect and of reason itself?

What if the reality is exactly as Solomon described it in the book of Ecclesiastes?

> When I applied my mind to know wisdom and to observe man's labor on earth—his eyes not seeing sleep day or night—then I saw all that God had done. No one can comprehend what goes on under the sun. Despite all his efforts to search it out, man cannot discover its meaning. Even if a wise man claims he knows, he cannot really comprehend it. …
>
> As you do not know the path of the wind, or how the body is formed in a mother's womb, so you cannot understand the work of God, the maker of all things.[24]

When we come face to face with the limitations of our human intellect, what should our response be? As we will see in the next two chapters, the way we answer this question has profound implications for the way we practice our faith and the way we respond to those whose beliefs and values differ from our own.

---

[23] Proverbs 3:5
[24] Ecclesiastes 8:16-17, 11:5

Appendix

A brief digression on Gödel's Incompleteness Theorems

In the early 1900s, mathematicians were in the midst of what is often called a "foundational crisis." Efforts to boil all of mathematics down to a set of basic axioms had been largely unsuccessful, as all such formulations had seemed to lead to inconsistencies and paradoxes.

In 1900, German mathematician David Hilbert had posed a sequence of 23 significant mathematical problems pertaining to a variety of topics throughout mathematics as it was developed at the time. To this day, some of Hilbert's problems remain unsolved while others have been resolved definitively.

The problem that is relevant to our discussion here is Hilbert's second problem, which sought to establish what appears on the surface to be a rather modest result: that the axioms of arithmetic—that is, the rules that govern addition and multiplication of whole numbers—are consistent. In other words, if these rules are applied properly, we should not be able to derive two results that contradict each other.

Hilbert's second problem was significant because Hilbert believed that the problem of establishing the consistency of mathematics as a whole could be reduced to that of establishing the consistency of arithmetic. In essence,

Hilbert believed that if we could find a way to put arithmetic on a firm logical foundation, then the rest of mathematics would follow suit.

Now fast forward to 1931, when Gödel dealt a serious blow to Hilbert's program by proving his famous incompleteness theorems. We learned earlier about Gödel's first theorem, which established that no axiom system that is robust enough to allow for basic arithmetic can be both consistent and complete. Gödel also showed that no axiom system can prove its own consistency. In other words, even if we are willing to sacrifice completeness for the sake of consistency, we cannot be sure that we are really getting the latter unless we appeal to additional axioms, or perhaps different axioms altogether.

This second observation is significant, because Gödel did not prove that basic arithmetic necessarily leads to inconsistencies. In fact, in 1936, German mathematician Gerhard Gentzen proved using other methods that the axioms of arithmetic *are* consistent. So, for those of you who were worried that your second-grade teacher was wrong, you can rest assured. And for those of you who were hoping to pawn off your mathematical shortcomings on the work of Gödel —well, better luck next time.

What Gödel did prove is that, in mathematics, we cannot have both completeness and consistency, regardless of what axioms we start with. We may be able to find a consistent set of axioms for arithmetic, but those axioms won't be able to prove everything about arithmetic—and much less everything about mathematics as a whole. So Hilbert's goal of reducing all of mathematics down to the axioms of arithmetic is, for all practical purposes, unattainable.

Chapter 3

Faith

For the past several years, I've had the privilege of being a part of an amazing group of men. We come from a variety of different religious backgrounds and experiences, but at one point or another, each of us has attended the nondenominational church that we now meet at one morning a week. Our occupations run the gamut from pastor to painter to glue salesman to web designer and everything in between. (For the record, I'm the nerd of the group.) Politically, some of us are gun-toting conservatives and others had the nerve to vote for Obama. (Twice.) We are different in so many ways, but what unites us is our commitment to pursue God together and to support each other through prayer and fellowship as we each navigate our own spiritual journey.

Some churches would call us a "small group," and I suppose that label is accurate to some extent. But we are different than any other small group that I've been a part of. For one thing, we've never done a formal study or worked through any kind of curriculum. And we don't really do "accountability" in the traditional sense of spending hours talking about all the ways we've messed up—in effect, helping each other discover new ways to sin. In fact, our meetings typically have no agenda other than talking about what's going on in our lives and joining together in prayer. Sometimes we sing a few songs and have communion. Other times we just laugh at the joys and frustrations of life. We have celebrated each other's successes and shared in each other's struggles. Bankruptcy. Broken marriages. Infidelity. Depression. Loneliness. Spiritual darkness. You name it; we've been there. It's no exaggeration to say that walking with these men has been one of the most profound spiritual experiences of my life.

Every now and then, someone new shows up at our group. Typically they don't last long. Between the talk of the crazy ways God has worked in our lives and the occasional profanities in our prayers, I think we have a way of scaring people away.

But, that being said, our group has picked up new members from time to time. Recently, two new men joined us, and they've returned several times, so I'm optimistic that they'll stay. We welcome anyone who is looking for the kind of fellowship we've discovered, and we've been blessed to have a number of guys take us up on that offer over the years.

A few years ago, an older gentleman named Don—he looked a bit like Santa Claus—showed up at our group. Right away, we knew there was something different about him (other than the white beard, of course). He knew his Bible cover to cover, but he also projected a certain sense of humility. Don didn't hesitate to talk about his own failures, and when he did, he seemed genuinely repentant. He was also quick to express his admiration for our group and the way we were pursuing God.

In many ways, Don embodied the kind of faith that we were longing for, the perfect combination of wisdom and humility. Don seemed to have it all figured out, and that was appealing to us. We were drawn to the certainty with which he held his views, and for several weeks we looked forward to hearing his insights into scripture and all things spiritual.

As time went on, however, we began to see a different side of Don. For instance, we learned that Don wasn't the only member of his church with a beard. In fact, every man had one—not by choice, but by edict of the church. Thankfully, the women were free from this requirement, but there were other rules for them. For starters, they had to cover their heads at church, wear skirts at all times, and remain silent during services. They were encouraged to marry young, and college was frowned upon. In Don's church, there were no birthdays, holidays, or anniversaries.

Personal photographs were taken as a sign of pride, and public sporting events were considered too worldly for God's people. Polo shirts were improper. And the list went on.

Over time, Don's presence at our meetings became more forceful, controlling, and uncomfortable. He began to criticize the way our group was structured and even the bibles that we used. He insisted that the New Living Translation was unacceptable and that we needed to get "real bibles"—King James Version of course. A few times, he "prophesied" over us. What started as friendly advice and suggestions from a fellow believer quickly became "words from the Lord," and it wasn't long before we realized that we had been duped.

As it turns out, Don was not who we thought he was. Behind the veneer of humble spirituality was an insecure and prideful man who used his knowledge of scripture to control and manipulate his followers. Don's church—or more accurately, cult—operated under a strict and comprehensive set of rules, all ostensibly rooted in scripture. Don was the ultimate biblicist. When asked if two followers of Christ could read the same passage of scripture and interpret it in different ways, his answer was an emphatic no. The natural consequence of this perspective was that if you disagreed with Don on just about anything, you were not a genuine follower of Christ.

Don's true colors shone through when we finally asked him to leave our group. His response: "You guys need me to lead you into the truth! Unless I teach you, you're lost! I can show you guys the way to salvation. If you don't accept it, you're going to hell!"

Looking back, we probably should have seen it coming. But a forceful presence like Don's can be disorienting and alluring at the same time. At times, our desire to make sense of God—to comprehend the incomprehensible—is so strong that it defies all logic and common sense. Case in point: In spite of what we eventually learned about Don, several of us still considered joining his church. In fact, one of our members did, only to return, wounded and defeated, a year and a half later.

Just about everyone who has contemplated the divine eventually runs head first into a sequence of terrifying questions. Questions like:

What do I have to do to please this God, and what happens if I don't?

Are my beliefs the right beliefs? What if I'm wrong?

Does God really love me? Am I good enough?

Is God's grace big enough to cover my mistakes?

In the end, am I going to be okay?

What makes these questions even more terrifying is the fact that, if we're honest with ourselves, none of us is 100% confident in our answers to them, and we probably can't ever be. Even the strongest believers have moments of doubt, times when we think:

Maybe I've got this all wrong. Maybe I'm only doing what I want to do, and I've convinced myself that it's what God wants too.

Maybe all of my beliefs are self-serving. Maybe this whole system I've constructed is just an elaborate ruse to make me feel better about myself.

Maybe God doesn't love me as much as I would like to believe He does.

Maybe I'm not good enough.

Maybe God's grace isn't big enough for someone like me.

Maybe I'm not going to be okay. Maybe I'm broken beyond repair.

Maybe I'm screwed.

Wrestling with these difficult questions is nothing short of exhausting, and it can be tempting to look for an easy way out. This is exactly what an authoritarian leader like Don provides.

It may seem strange to describe as an "easy way out" a legalistic church led by a controlling patriarch who demands full obedience to his decrees. In the midst of oppressive doubt and uncertainty, however, trading liberty for a sense of security can seem like an appealing option—even if the security offered is only an illusion.

What Don and others like him offer is a prescription for how to be right with God. If you do this and don't do that, read this bible instead of the other one, pray the right prayers, believe the right doctrine, worship the right way, and—perhaps most importantly—submit to my authority and the authority of the church, then—and only then—will you be okay.

The problem with this prescription is that it has absolutely nothing to do with the gospel of Jesus Christ. Its appeal rests in the fact that it boils following God down to a set of rules—something manageable and under our control. An authoritarian, legalistic approach to spirituality *does* require faith, but not in God. The faith required is in a person or institution—in essence, faith by proxy. Human beings and human institutions may be flawed, but they are tangible. And it is easier to put our faith in things that we can see or touch than to lay our souls directly at the feet of a God who is beyond our comprehension.

Authoritarianism, and its manifestations in religious and political institutions, has been studied extensively by social scientists. One of the foremost experts in this area is Canadian psychologist Bob Altemeyer. His book, *The Authoritarians*,[25] provides a summary of more than 40 years of research on authoritarian followers and the leaders that inspire them.

Before I delve into Altemeyer's research, I need to give a disclaimer. First, Altemeyer does not fit the mold of the types of authors typically cited in books like this. He is a confessed agnostic who is quite critical of conservative politics and religion. Altemeyer himself acknowledges that some may question his conclusions due to this fact. For instance, he writes:

> Because religion is such an opinion-based topic, I had better lay my own cards on the table. I was raised a Catholic and was a strong believer until age 21. After searching other religions I became a "None" and then an agnostic… I don't think any of this has affected the answers people have given to my surveys… But as always, you will be the judge of that.[26]

One response to Altemeyer's personal political and religious views would be to discount his contributions as biased and agenda-driven. However, I'd like us to resist that temptation. As Richard Mouw writes:

---

[25] Altemeyer, B. (2006). *The Authoritarians*. Available at http://home.cc.umanitoba.ca/~altemey/
[26] Ibid., p. 141.

No matter how antagonistic a perspective may be toward things that we hold precious, we should be willing to at least listen to the criticisms. And sometimes we might even learn something helpful from those criticisms. … The Lord often sends strange teachers our way. We need to be open to the lessons he wants us to learn from them. [27]

So with that perspective in mind, let's take a look at what Altemeyer's research reveals. We'll focus primarily on authoritarian *followers*—for our purposes, average everyday members of churches with authoritarian tendencies.

What do we know about authoritarian followers? First, they are dogmatic, meaning that they hold their beliefs with a "relatively unchangeable, unjustified certainty." [28] Authoritarian followers, having absorbed many of their beliefs from others, may not know *why* they believe what they believe. Because of this, they tend to avoid situations where their beliefs may be challenged. This is largely accomplished by associating primarily with others who share their beliefs.

When an authoritarian follower is challenged about their beliefs, they are likely to repeat stock arguments or sound bites they have heard from their leaders. If these

---

[27] Mouw, R. (2010). *Uncommon decency: Christian civility in an uncivil world.* 2nd ed. Downers Grove, IL: InterVarsity Press. (p. 62)
[28] Ibid., p. 92.

arguments are not convincing (which is often the case), authoritarian followers may "simply insist [they] are right and walk away, clutching [their] beliefs more tightly than ever."[29]

Authoritarian followers are particularly susceptible to confirmation bias and post-hoc rationalization. When core beliefs are called into question, authoritarians tend to seek assurance from supportive sources rather than examining the evidence on both sides of the issue.

As one might suspect, authoritarian followers tend to appeal to authority rather than engage in independent, critical thought. Authoritarians have just as many doubts about their beliefs as others, but they are taught to suppress these doubts. As Altemeyer puts it, "the doubts remain, but are enormously covered up."[30]

Authoritarians insist on and trust in their leaders to provide a complete and consistent picture of God—even though, as we discussed in the last chapter, such a picture is likely beyond the capabilities of human reason and intellect. Nevertheless, the dominant tendency among authoritarians is to mangle the puzzle pieces so that they all fit together in some way, often ignoring, explaining away, or simply denying the inevitable inconsistencies that result from this process.

---

[29] Ibid., p. 93.
[30] Ibid., p. 139.

The ability of authoritarians to rationalize and deny inconsistencies carries over to their personal lives as well. Authoritarians have what Altemeyer refers to as "highly compartmentalized minds" and often hold contradictory positions on a variety of issues. According to Altemeyer, "authoritarians' ideas are poorly integrated with each other" and "they don't seem to scan for self-consistency as much as most people do."[31] Because of this, authoritarians tend to hold double standards and act in ways that most outside observers would view as hypocritical. Even so, authoritarians often view themselves as being considerably more moral and generally better people than others with different beliefs. At the same time, authoritarians are "sure they are less self-righteous than most people."[32] In fact, if you described the negative traits associated with authoritarianism to an authoritarian (as Altemeyer has done in his experiments), they would likely think you were talking about someone else.

Authoritarians place a high value on certainty. They find joy, comfort, and security in knowing—ostensibly beyond the shadow of a doubt—that they have the right answers. For this reason, questions are a serious threat to all that authoritarians hold dear.

---

[31] Ibid., pp. 81-82.
[32] Ibid., p. 87.

According to Altemeyer, authoritarians are "chronically frightened." They view the world as a dangerous place, full of evil forces that must be resisted. The security that authoritarians find in certainty tends to mask a much deeper sense of doubt, anxiety, and fear. In other words, it is a false and fragile sense of security that provides some level of comfort but is constantly at risk of being disrupted by differing viewpoints and perspectives. Because of this, authoritarians tend to be highly defensive.

None of this paints a particularly positive picture of authoritarian believers, and so one would hope that such folks are the exception rather than the rule. Unfortunately, the research shows that among fundamentalist and evangelical Christians, the opposite is true; indeed, authoritarianism is highly prevalent among these groups.

If there is any silver lining here, it is that the kind of social psychological research in which Altemeyer and others like him specialize is good for making accurate conclusions about tendencies among *groups* of people, but can miss nuances within *individuals*. Thus, not *all* authoritarians exhibit *all* of the traits associated with authoritarianism. Likewise, not all fundamentalist or evangelical Christians are authoritarians. This last point is particularly salient because I suspect that many of the readers of this book would describe themselves as evangelicals. If you are someone who thinks of yourself in these terms, please know that I am not trying to alienate you or make any unwarranted assumptions about the way you practice your faith. I am simply attempting to highlight some of the traps that all Christians can fall into, and that certain groups of Christians tend to fall into more often than others.

Earlier, we made note of Altemeyer's critical views of conservative politics and religion. However, in spite of this potential bias, his claims are remarkably consistent with the Barna group research we considered in Chapter 1, which is detailed by Kinnaman and Lyons in the book *Unchristian*.[33] In fact, Altemeyer's research suggests that the perceptions of Christians held by those outside the church are at some level rooted in reality, and that authoritarianism may be the major culprit.

Kinnaman and Lyons found that outsiders perceived Christians to be hypocritical and judgmental—traits that, as we have seen, are often associated with authoritarianism.

What about the perception that Christians are agenda-driven, especially in their approach to evangelism? Altemeyer notes that authoritarians are particularly

---

[33] Kinnaman, D., & Lyons, G. (2007). *Unchristian: What a new generation really thinks about Christianity… and why it matters.* Grand Rapids, MI: Baker Books.

zealous, and that "fundamentalists usually believe they have an *obligation* to try to convert others." [34]

Or how about Christians being sheltered? Altemeyer writes:

> I have discovered in my investigations that, by and large, high [authoritarian] students had simply missed many of the experiences that might have lowered their authoritarianism. ... They had contentedly traveled around on short leashes in relatively small, tight, safe circles all their lives. [35]

Writing specifically about fundamentalism, Altemeyer notes:

> I want to emphasize also that all of the above is based on studies in which, if the opposite were true instead, that would have been shown. This is not just "somebody's opinion." It's what the fundamentalists themselves said and did. And it adds up to a truly depressing bottom line.[36]

At some point, we must take a long, hard look at the church—and ourselves—and acknowledge that if it looks like a duck and quacks like a duck, then it probably is a duck—or in this case, authoritarianism.

---

[34] Ibid., p. 126.
[35] Ibid., p. 61.
[36] Ibid., p. 140.

I want to again reiterate that none of these general patterns apply to *all* Christians (or *all* evangelicals, or *all* fundamentalists). Furthermore, I suspect that many Christians practice an authoritarian faith simply because it is all they know, or because they have been led to believe that the characteristics associated with authoritarianism are part and parcel of Christian orthodoxy. There is, however, another way.

In 1982, psychologists Daniel Batson and Larry Ventis introduced the *quest* construct to describe a type of religious belief and practice characterized by an open-ended search for truth that places value on doubt and uncertainty. Questers are in essence the opposite of authoritarians. In contrast to authoritarians, who tend to think less complexly about religious issues and have difficulty accepting the possible validity of contradictory beliefs,[37] questers think about religious issues in more complex ways, allowing room for multiple interpret-tations.[38] When faith is viewed as a quest, beliefs remain open to change and questions are not only accepted but embraced.

---

[37] Pancer, S. M., Jackson, L. M., Hunsberger, B., Pratt, M. W., & Lea, J. (1995). Religious orthodoxy and the complexity of thought about religious and nonreligious issues. *Journal of Personality*, 63(2), 213-232.

[38] Batson, C. D., & Raynor-Prince, L. (1983). Religious orientation and complexity of thought about existential concerns. *Journal for the Scientific Study of Religion*, 22(1), 38-50.

Some questers are marked by religious angst, frequently changing religious views, and agnosticism or rejection of orthodox Christian beliefs. But others quest while remaining fundamentally committed to the core beliefs of Christianity. If fact, questers are not, as a group, less likely than others to hold orthodox Christian beliefs.[39] One pair of researchers put it this way:

> Persons within a religious worldview, in this case Christianity, can be tentative, curious, accepting of other Christian faiths, and not beholden to Biblical literalism. These are Quest-like attributes which do not appear to be incompatible with having reached some fundamental metaphysical conclusions (e.g., Jesus is the Son of God).[40]

There are, of course, some challenges that all questers must face. First and foremost, questing requires one to abandon of the sense of security that comes from "knowing" the answers. As we have discussed, this security is nothing more than a mirage, but it is comforting nonetheless. To quest, one must leave behind the baggage of spiritual pride and embrace the terrifying yet beautiful reality of knowing God for who He really is, and

---

[39] Batson, C. D., & Schoenrade, P. A. (1991). Measuring religion as quest: 1) Validity concerns. *Journal for the Scientific Study of Religion, 30*(4), 416-429; Batson, D. C., & Ventis, W. L. (1982). *The religious experience: A social-psychological perspective.* New York, NY: Oxford University Press.

[40] Beck, R., & Jessup, R. K. (2004). The multidimensional nature of quest motivation. *Journal of Psychology and Theology, 32*(4), 283-294.

not just who we want Him to be. As James McDonald writes:

> God is not safe and He will not be squeezed into some neat, respectable Sunday discussion. … No. To know God at all is to watch Him explode any box we put Him in with His terror, majesty and indescribable wonder. [41]

To know this God, and to allow ourselves to be known by Him, is the ultimate in humility. Only by putting to death our desire to contain God within the confines of our human minds can we begin to experience the depths of His love and mercy. As Paul writes in Ephesians:

> And I pray that you, being rooted and established in love, may have power, together with all the Lord's holy people, to grasp how wide and long and high and deep is the love of Christ, and to know this love that surpasses knowledge—that you may be filled to the measure of all the fullness of God. [42]

Love that surpasses knowledge: this is the fruit of knowing God and seeking him with humility.

The perfect love we find in the person of Christ is utterly incompatible with authoritarianism because it undermines the fear that drives authoritarianism. As John writes:

---

[41] MacDonald, J. (2005). *Gripped by the greatness of God.* Chicago, IL: Moody Publishers. (p. 13)
[42] Ephesians 3:17b-19

There is no fear in love. But perfect love drives out fear, because fear has to do with punishment. The one who fears is not made perfect in love.

We love because he first loved us. Whoever claims to love God yet hates a brother or sister is a liar. For whoever does not love their brother and sister, whom they have seen, cannot love God, whom they have not seen. And he has given us this command: Anyone who loves God must also love their brother and sister. [43]

According to John, loving our brothers and sisters is a prerequisite for loving God. But, as we will see in the next chapter, this is easier said than done—especially for those wed to authoritarianism.

---

[43] 1 John 4:18-21

Chapter 4

Love

For more than 15 years now, I've called West Michigan home, which means that I'm quite well acquainted with the conservative side of both politics and religion.

Grand Rapids is the world headquarters of the Christian Reformed Church, and my alma mater, Calvin College, is one of the flagship educational institutions of that particular denomination. In spite of this fact, I've never really attended a Christian Reformed church. In fact, my wife and I, even going back to our college days, have attended big nondenominational churches.

One of the churches we attended for a while during college was Calvary Church, which was at the time led by Ed Dobson. Over the years, we've had the privilege of hearing Ed preach a number of times, first at Calvary, and then as a guest at Ada Bible Church, and more recently at Mars Hill Bible Church, where his son Kent is now the senior teaching pastor.

We've also had the privilege—and it seems both odd and entirely appropriate to call it that—of watching Ed's journey as his body has slowly succumbed to ALS (Lou Gerhig's Disease). When we first heard Ed preach back in the late 1990s, he was energetic and full of life. Now, a little more than a decade after he was diagnosed, Ed is gaunt, weak, and frail. His voice is shaky, his speech is slow and slurred, and his arms are basically useless. And yet, in spite of—or perhaps because of—the disease that has ravaged his body, Ed Dobson has an air about him that is nothing short of inspiring. Ed projects a rare and authentic combination of honesty, contentment, joy, gratitude, humor, and raw emotion. I am deeply moved every time I hear him speak.

And yet Ed Dobson is not without his critics. In fact, back in 2008, he did something that was nothing short of anathema to many of his more conservative peers: he voted for Barack Obama.

News first broke of Dobson's support for Obama in a *Grand Rapids Press* article published in December of 2008.[44] What was really a passing comment in a larger story drew a significant amount of attention and ire from some Christian conservatives.

In a follow-up article, one of Dobson's colleagues at Cornerstone University (at the time, Dobson was serving a one-year stint as Vice President of Spiritual Formation),

---

[44] Honey, C. (2008, December 25). Walking the walk. *The Grand Rapids Press.*

said that "he wished Dobson had not made his vote public" and that it "was not germane to the Jesus lifestyle." [45] (More on that shortly.)

Pastor Matt Trewhella—whose *Missionaries to the Preborn* group is known for their protest signs featuring graphic images of aborted babies—wrote the following:

> Sadly, men like Dobson … and their ilk are corrupting Christian young people. They target the young. … Think how many lives he will corrupt. …
>
> When a Christian leader boasts about voting for Barack Obama he has apostatized. Christianity opposes the killing of the preborn and the legitimizing of sodomy. Always has. As a student of church history, I can assure you American Christianity is an aberration, it is not the real deal. [46]

Dobson may well have agreed with Trewhella on this last point about American Christianity. After all, the larger story to which I alluded earlier was Dobson's year-long commitment to live, as much as possible, the way Jesus would have lived. For all of 2008, Dobson had adhered strictly to Jewish customs, traditions, and dietary laws. He had also immersed himself in the teachings of Jesus by

---

[45] Honey, C. (2009, January 10). Critics say Dobson's 'pursuit of Jesus' veered off course. *The Grand Rapids Press*.

[46] Trewhella, M. (2009, January 28). Does anyone finish the race anymore? Retrieved from http://www.missionariestopreborn.com/msmlg1-09.pdf

listening to an audio recording of the four gospels at least once each week. [47]

By the time Dobson made his decision to support Obama, he had listened to the gospels dozens of times. He had reflected on themes in Jesus' teaching, including: treatment of the poor, marginalized, and oppressed; treatment of one's enemies; and commitment to peacemaking. He had also wrestled with the issue that was most problematic, both to him and many of his critics: abortion. In the end, he concluded the following:

> I am concerned about those within the conservative movement whose only concern is with the unborn. I agree with them. I stand with them. I support them. But I want to know why in the world they seem not to care about those who are *already* born.
>
> So I plan to vote for Senator Obama. Even though I disagree with him on the issue of abortion, being pro-life is a whole lot more than being concerned about abortion alone! [48]

Describing election day, Dobson writes:

> Inside, my heart was beating really fast. For the first time in my life, I was going to vote for a Democrat, and I wasn't sure how I felt about it. I knew that my vote for

---

[47] Dobson, E. (2009). *The year of living like Jesus.* Grand Rapids, MI: Zondervan.
[48] Ibid., p. 244.

> Senator Obama would be profoundly misunderstood by my conservative friends. ... But I made a commitment to try to live out Jesus' teachings, and to the best of my knowledge I was making a vote in keeping with that. ...
>
> I voted for Senator Obama because I felt that he, more than any other candidate, best represented the teachings of Jesus. [49]

Dobson was right to have anticipated the criticism. After all, the role of evangelicals in the 2008 election had been widely discussed, with many on both sides of the aisle expressing strong opinions about the compatibility of traditional Christian beliefs with the views of then-Senator Obama.

I remember a particularly strongly worded letter to the editor, in which the author asserted that "Christian Democrat is any oxymoron," that Jesus "wouldn't ever vote for a Democrat," and that those who disagree with this position "do not have Jesus in their heart."[50]

My response to this is: Really? Being a Republican—and believing that Jesus would have also been one—is now a requirement of authentic Christian faith?

Unfortunately, many evangelicals who fall to the left of center, either politically or theologically, face similar

---

[49] Ibid., pp. 245, 247.

[50] Lewis, J. (2008, July 25). Reflect on the Word [Letter to the editor]. *The Grand Rapids Press.*

condemnation. Rachel Held Evans mourns this reality, writing:

> As a young evangelical myself, I confess I have grown tired…no, weary…of responding to comments [about fellow evangelicals], only to be discounted and disparaged for believing the earth is more than 6,000 years old, for voting for Democrats from time to time, and for daring to serve communion to gays and lesbians. *The fact that I can affirm the Nicene and Apostle's creeds, that I am an imperfect but devoted follower of Jesus Christ, that I am passionate about spreading the gospel, and I believe the Bible is the inspired and authoritative Word of God, and still my evangelical credentials are constantly being questioned and debated reveals just how narrow evangelicalism has become.* [51]

There are, of course, those who seek to reverse the evangelical trend toward exclusivity. Rob Bell, who served under Ed Dobson at Calvary Church until leaving to found Mars Hill Bible Church, is among them.

In 2011, Bell wrote a little book called *Love Wins*. [52] Ultimately, the book unleashed a firestorm that made the Dobson-Obama incident seem like child's play.

In the case of *Love Wins*, the controversy started a month before the release of the book, with the posting of a video

---

[51] Held Evans, R. (2012). The real 'evangelical disaster'. Retrieved from http://rachelheldevans.com/blog/real-evangelical-disaster

[52] Bell, R. (2011). *Love wins: A book about heaven, hell, and the fate of every person who ever lived.* New York, NY: Harper-Collins.

trailer in which Bell told a story about an art show held at Mars Hill and a particular piece featuring a quote from Mahatma Gandhi. As Bell described it:

> Lots of people found this piece compelling. They'd stop and sort of stare at it and take it in or reflect on it, but not everybody found it that compelling. Somewhere in the course of the art show, somebody attached a handwritten note to the piece, and on the note, they had written, "Reality check: He's in hell."

Bell then went on to ask several provocative questions:

> Gandhi's in hell? He is? And someone knows this for sure, and felt the need to let the rest of us know? Will only a few select people make it to heaven, and will billions and billions of people burn forever in hell? And if that's the case, how do you become one of the few? ... And then there is the question behind the questions—the real question: What is God like? ... How could that God ever be good? How could that God ever be trusted? And how could that ever be good news? [53]

While Bell stopped short of explicitly answering these questions in the video, what he did say led many to

---

[53] Bell, R. (2011). *Love wins.* – Available March 15 [Video file]. Retrieved from http://vimeo.com/20272585

believe that he was endorsing *universalism*—that is, the belief that all will eventually be saved. [54]

Four days after the promotional video was posted, blogger Justin Taylor published the first of many blog posts debating Bell's views and his standing within the evangelical community. Taylor's post was entitled, "Rob Bell: Universalist?" In it, he wrote, "It is unspeakably sad when those called to be ministers of the Word distort the gospel and deceive the people of God with false doctrine." With regard to Bell's doctrinal position, he wrote, "I'm glad that Rob Bell has the integrity to lay his cards on the table about universalism. It seems that this is not just optimism about the fate of those who haven't heard the Good News, but ... full-blown hell-is-empty-everyone-gets-saved universalism." [55]

---

[54] Bell's views became clearer when *Love Wins* was published. To some extent, *Love Wins* can be viewed as an endorsement of universalism, although I would argue that to classify Bell as a universalist is an oversimplification of his position. If Bell is a universalist, his brand of universalism is profoundly Christ-centered. Moreover, Bell seems more interested in promoting the *possibility* of eventual universal reconciliation than the *certainty* of this outcome. (My Master's thesis on this topic, *The Love Wins controversy: A case study in religiosity and social identity*, is available at http://gvsu.edu/s/cS.)

[55] Taylor, J. (2011, February 26). Rob Bell: Universalist? Retrieved from http://thegospelcoalition.org/blogs/justintaylor/2011/02/26/rob-bell-universalist/

Pastor and author John Piper was more succinct, tweeting a few hours later, "Farewell, Rob Bell." [56] As Jon Meacham would later write in *Time* magazine, Piper seemed to be "unilaterally attempting to evict Bell from the Evangelical community." [57] Keep in mind that all of this happened a full month before *Love Wins* was scheduled to be released.

After his book was published, critics [58] labeled Bell a false prophet, a "rock-star pastor" who doesn't believe "the whole Bible" and has "made up his own religion." One critic wrote that Bell "has become big enough in his own estimation to declare that the creator and upholder of this vast universe has no right to send people to hell." Others labeled Bell as one who lacks discernment, waters down God's word, suppresses the truth, rejects the authority of the Bible, and "cheats" people through "philosophy and empty deceit." For this, one critic concluded that Bell was subject to "wrath [that] no denial on his part will enable him to escape."

Bell's message was described as a "feel good gospel," one that is characterized by a "totally inclusive Jesus" and contains "no judgment and thus no hell." One critic called

---

[56] http://twitter.com/#!/JohnPiper/statuses/41590656421863424
[57] Meacham, J. (2011). Is hell dead? *Time, 177*(16), 38. Retrieved from http://www.time.com/time/magazine/article/0,9171,2065289,00.html
[58] The quotes I have included here are from an analysis of letters to the editor in my Master's thesis, available at http://gvsu.edu/s/cS.

Bell's positions "misguided, harmful and contrary to the clear teaching of Scripture and the great standards of the Christian faith." Another used stronger language, writing that "Rob Bell's latest assertions are as old as Satan's."

My point in giving these examples—and there are countless others as well—is not to enter into a debate about politics or theology, but rather to illustrate the simple fact that Christians often seem utterly incapable of managing their differences in a way that exhibits anything close to grace.

Part of the problem is black and white, either/or thinking. It is, as Rabbi Jonathan Sacks puts it, the belief that:

> If I am right, you are wrong. If what I believe is the truth, then your belief, which differs from mine, must be an error from which you must be converted, cured and saved. From this flowed some of the great crimes of history... [59]

Even more devastating is the dehumanization of those who differ from us. As Sacks puts it:

> One belief, more than any other (to quote a phrase of Isaiah Berlin's) is responsible for the slaughter of individuals on the altars of the great historical ideals. It is the belief that those who do not share my faith—or my

---

[59] Sacks, J. (2003). *The dignity of difference: How to avoid the clash of civilizations.* New York, NY: Continuum. (p. 50)

race or my ideology—do not share my humanity. At best they are second-class citizens. At worst they forfeit the sanctity of life itself. They are the unsaved, the unbelievers, the infidel, the unredeemed; they stand outside the circle of salvation. If faith is what makes us human, then those who do not share my faith are less than fully human. [60]

Why are we so quick to demonize—and indeed, even dehumanize—those whose beliefs are different than our own? One answer lies in Sacks suggestion that "faith is what makes us human." Or, to paraphrase: faith is central to our *identity* as human beings.

Social scientists have come to view the concept of identity as essential to understanding the complexity of human interactions, particularly in conflict situations. Up until the 1960s, conflict was viewed primarily as a competition for scarce resources. In other words, both parties in a conflict want something that only one can have. This view is in many ways consistent with the narrative in the book of James, where the author writes:

> What causes fights and quarrels among you? Don't they come from the desires that battle within you? You desire but do not have, so you kill. You covet but you cannot get what you want, so you quarrel and fight. [61]

---

[60] Ibid., pp. 45-46.
[61] James 4:1-2a

But the desires that battle within us are not simply for tangible things like money, power, and recognition. There is a deeper desire that plays an equally important role, and that is the desire to belong. As it turns out, we tend to derive a fair amount of our sense of self-worth from the social groups with which we identify. These social identifications help define who we are, which is why we often describe ourselves in terms of the groups to which we belong.

For example, I am a professor—a member of academia. I'm also a husband, a father, and an aspiring Christ-follower. I happen to be white, male, and heterosexual. All of these things in some way define who I am—and consequently, who I am not. I am not a plumber. I am not single. I am neither black, Muslim, nor gay.

The reason all of this matters is that, as human beings, we have a tendency to categorize others based on the extent to which they are similar to and/or different from us. We divide the world into "us" and "them," creating what social psychologists refer to as *ingroups* and *outgroups*. But what happens when our ingroups and outgroups collide?

Take, for example, a politically conservative Christian—call him Conservative Cal. What happens when Conservative Cal meets Lucy Liberal and is surprised to learn that Lucy is also a professing Christian? Is Lucy in or out? Is she an "us" or a "them"?

If Cal looks only at Lucy's religious beliefs, she will fall squarely within his ingroup. But if Cal looks only at Lucy's political views, the opposite is true. (Lucy, by the way, faces the same dilemma in attempting to categorize Cal.) The problem is that Lucy's identity, like Cal's, is multidimensional. She considers herself to be both a Christian and a liberal, and she sees no inherent contradiction in the two. In fact, Lucy might even believe that liberalism is a necessary consequence of a Christian worldview (as the "Jesus was a liberal" bumper stickers would suggest), and that Cal is the one whose beliefs are inconsistent.

If Cal and Lucy are going to have any kind of meaningful interactions pertaining to politics or religion, each will need to find a way to reconcile the contradictions they perceive in the other's identity. What the research shows is that their ability to do so will depend on the complexity of their thinking about their own identities.

Those who conceptualize their identities in less complex ways are likely to have narrowly defined ingroups. They view identity as one-dimensional and belonging as an all or nothing proposition. It is this kind of thinking that leads to statements like "_____ Christian is an oxymoron," where one can fill in the blank with any number of descriptors—for example: rich, poor, gay, homophobic, conservative, liberal, capitalist, socialist, universalist, Calvinist, Catholic, Protestant, and the list goes on.

Of course, this kind of simplistic categorization forces one to deny self-professed aspects of the other's identity in order to fit them neatly into exactly one box: "us" or "them." So, for instance, the gay Christian must not really be gay (perhaps he is just confused), or must not really be a Christian. When reality makes certain denials untenable—for example, it's hard to argue that Ed Dobson didn't *really* vote for *Obama*—all that is left is to attack what remains, which is, tragically but frequently, one's religious identification. So Ed Dobson is an apostate who is corrupting Christian young people, Rob Bell is a heretic whose words are comparable to those of Satan, and anyone who believes differently than I do needs to be corrected or risk endless torment in hell.

It grieves me to think that this kind of counterfeit gospel— a gospel of exclusion rather than inclusion—is what passes for the good news of Jesus Christ among many groups of well-intentioned believers.

As one might expect, the problem is not with the religious teachings themselves—which, across most religions, are overwhelmingly prosocial—but rather the way these beliefs are held. Gordon Allport, one of the 20th century's most prominent researchers on the psychology of religion, noted that "there is something about religion that makes for prejudice, and something about it that unmakes prejudice."[62] A type of prejudice this is particularly relevant to our discussion here is rooted in *religious enthnocentrism*—that is, the making of us-them distinctions on the basis of religious beliefs, and the resulting actions to preserve these distinctions by castigating, marginalizing, or ostracizing those who don't fit neatly into the narrowly defined ingroup.

Research shows that enthnocentrism is most common among fundamentalists. Altemeyer argued that fundamentalists in particular "tend to have a very small 'us' and quite a large 'them' when it comes to faith."[63] Again, the issue here is not the beliefs themselves, but rather the attitude that these beliefs are the only ones that are fundamentally correct, and that those who disagree must be corrected, converted, or excluded. Put another way, it is the authoritarian aspect of fundamentalism that leads to the religious ethnocentrism that is at the root of so many of the intergroup tensions that plague religious communities.

---

[62] Allport, G. W. (1966). The religious context of prejudice. *Journal for the Scientific Study of Religion, 5*, 447-457.
[63] Altemeyer, B. (2003). Why do religious fundamentalists tend to be prejudiced? *The International Journal for the Psychology of Religion, 13*(1). (p. 27)

Compounding the problem is the fact that religious identification is often more powerful than identification with other social groups, owing in part to the fact that religious group membership is often considered eternal.[64] Consequently, issues involving the afterlife and salvation can evoke a particularly defensive response.

Ultimately, what folks like Ed Dobson and Rob Bell threaten is the *distinctiveness* and *superiority* of the religious ingroup. For all our talk about grace and equality in the eyes of God, I fear that some Christians are all too comfortable drawing the line between in and out, us and them, saved and unsaved, heaven-bound and hell-bound. Regardless of our views on the inclusiveness of salvation, should we not as Christians mirror the desire of our Creator, "who wants all people to be saved and to come to a knowledge of the truth"?[65]

Instead, the research shows that those who have a strong sense of religious identification are likely to: (1) resist attempts to increase the inclusiveness of the ingroup;[66] (2)

---

[64] Ysseldyk, R., Matheson, K., & Anisman, H. (2010). Religiosity as identity: Toward an understanding of religion from a social identity perspective. *Personality and Social Psychology Review, 14*(1), 60-71.

[65] 1 Timothy 2:4; Rob Bell made this same point in *Love Wins*, writing: "Whatever objections a person might have to this story, and there are many, one has to admit that it is fitting, proper, and Christian to long for it." (Ibid., p. 111)

[66] Roccas, S., Sagiv, L., Scwhartz, S., Halevy, N., & Eidelson, R. (2008). Toward a unifying model of identification with groups: Integrating

exhibit higher levels of ingroup bias when the distinctiveness of their perceived ingroup is threatened;[67] (3) react strongly to distinctiveness threats in an attempt to restore distinctiveness;[68] and (4) ostracize or marginalize ingroup members who threaten group distinctiveness or blur group boundaries.[69]

All of this suggests a disturbing reality: for those of us whose religious beliefs are central to our identities, there is a persistent temptation to derive some aspect of our self-worth from the fact that we are saved and others are not. We may pay lip service to grace and rightly attribute our salvation to the redemptive work of Christ, but if our attitude toward those outside of our faith carries even a hint of condemnation, we have missed the point.

The antidote to the poison of superiority is not anything-goes, unfettered relativism, but rather humility. As Rob Bell puts it:

---

theoretical perspectives. *Personality and Social Psychology Review, 12*(3), 280-306.

[67] Schmid, K., Hewstone, M., Tausch, N., Cairns, E., & Hughes, J. (2009). Antecedents and consequences of social identity complexity: Intergroup contact, distinctiveness threat, and outgroup attitudes. *Personality and Social Psychology Bulletin, 35*(8), 1085-1098.

[68] Jetten, J., Spears, R., & Postmes, T. (2004). Intergroup distinctiveness and differentiation: A meta-analytic integration. *Journal of Personality and Social Psychology, 86*(6), 862-879.

[69] Ysseldyk, R., Matheson, K., & Anisman, H. (2010). Religiosity as identity: Toward an understanding of religion from a social identity perspective. *Personality and Social Psychology Review, 14*(1), 60-71.

You can believe something with so much conviction that you'd die for that belief, *and yet in the exact same moment*, you can also say, "I could be wrong..."

This is because conviction and humility, like faith and doubt, are not opposites; they're dance partners. It's possible to hold your faith with open hands, living with great conviction and yet at the same time humbly admitting that your knowledge and perspective will always be limited.[70]

If this point of view sounds decidedly quest-like, it's because it is. And perhaps not surprisingly, research shows that questers are among the least prejudiced of all religious believers. It seems that the tentativeness, curiosity, and complexity inherent in questers' thinking about religious beliefs extends to the complexity of their social identifications as well. As a consequence, questers tend to have highly inclusive ingroups—a stark contrast to authoritarians.

When I put all of these observations together—how intellectual pride leads to authoritarianism, which in turn foments prejudice and religious ethnocentrism, and how questers tend to be largely immune to these social ills—I find myself convinced that what the church needs right now is a critical mass of believers who are willing to embrace an open, questing faith that flows from a proper

---

[70] Bell, R. (2013). *What we talk about when we talk about God.* New York, NY: HarperOne. (p. x)

understanding of the richness of God's love for all of humanity and its expression through the free and freeing gift of grace.

In the next few chapters, we'll explore some of the nuts and bolts of what this kind of faith might look like in practice.

Part II

The Way of Humility

Chapter 5

Humility

We've spent the last few chapters talking about the problems of intellectual pride, authoritarianism, and ethnocentrism. But now it is time for us to move beyond theory and tackle a very practical question: how does one live out a faith that is not plagued by these ills? Or, stated more succinctly, what are the habits of spiritual humility?

To attempt to provide the beginnings of an answer to this question, I'd like to focus on a few simple phrases—words that I believe are essential to the pursuit of spiritual humility.

You see, words are powerful. Scripture calls us to speak the truth and to be transformed by the renewing of our minds. In Romans, Paul follows this latter admonition with another one: "Do not think of yourself more highly than you ought, but rather think of yourself with sober judgment, in accordance with the faith God has distributed to each of you."[71] For Paul, the renewing of one's mind seems to go hand in hand with humility, which

---

[71] Romans 12:3

requires an honest and appropriately sober view of one's importance and abilities. The renewed mind clings to truth and, in doing so, must be willing to admit its own limitations. And so, first and foremost, the renewed mind must be willing to say, "I don't know."

I distinctly remember—and it was probably 15 years ago now—going on a long run with my dad and being completely caught off guard when a bumper sticker on a car unexpectedly steered our conversation toward a sequence of spiritual question like, "How could I ever be happy in heaven if I knew that my loved ones were being tortured in hell?" As a good Calvinist (at the time), I'm sure that the answer I gave had something to do with God's sovereignty and the sufficiency of Christ and so forth. But I'm also quite certain that it was thoroughly unsatisfying to my dad. You see, he wasn't looking for an intellectual explanation. His question was one of emotion and practicality, not one that could be addressed by explicating theological principles.

Looking back, I'm not sure that I even believed the answers I gave. How could I have? There are some questions that simply evade any kind of satisfying human explanation. There are some questions for which the only honest answer is, "I don't know."

In her book, *Help, Thanks, Wow*, Anne LaMott provides an incredibly honest and poignant description of this reality. She writes:

> Human lives are hard, even those of health and privilege, and don't make much sense. ... God tells Job, who wants an explanation for all his troubles, "You wouldn't understand."
>
> And we don't understand a lot of things. ...
>
> If I were going to begin practicing the presence of God for the first time today, it would help to begin by admitting the three most terrible truths of our existence: that we are so ruined, and so loved, and in charge of so little.[72]

Humility requires a giving up, a letting go, an admission that we are not as in control as we would like to be. Humility also requires us to dispose of the myth that God demands definitive answers, and that uncertainty is evidence of a weak faith (a rather ironic perspective, as certainty negates the very need for faith!). Finally, we must put aside the anthropocentric and patronizing notion that questions—particularly those that remain unanswered—pose a threat to God's reputation and therefore must be dealt with swiftly. Describing this response, Daniel Taylor writes:

---

[72] LaMott, A. (2012). *Help, thanks, wow: The three essential prayers.* New York, NY: Penguin Group. (pp. 23-24, 27)

> Supposedly they are protecting God, an almost humorous notion if its consequences were not so hurtful. Apparently God is fragile, His feelings easily hurt, sort of like Mr. Snuffleupagus on "Sesame Street" who feels sad and frustrated when people don't believe he exists. Actually, they are protecting themselves, their view of the world, and their sense of security. [73]

*Them*selves.

Their view of the world.

Their sense of security.

This really isn't about God at all, is it?

One of the less admirable traits of fallen humanity is a tendency to clothe self-serving motives in a veil of nobility. This rationalization may, and often does, occur on a subconscious level. In fact, we probably lie to ourselves as much as we do to others, apparently subscribing to the wisdom of George Constanza from Seinfeld: "Jerry, just remember, it's not a lie if you believe it."

Many well-intentioned Christ-followers honestly believe that their faith requires them to be prepared to answer any and all questions posed by skeptics, nonbelievers, atheists, agnostics, members of other faiths, and even

---

[73] Taylor, D. (1992). *The myth of certainty: The reflective Christian and the risk of commitment.* Downers Grove, IL: InterVarsity Press. (p. 30)

other Christians who belong to the wrong denomination or subscribe to the wrong theology. Scores of books have been written on understanding, explaining, and defending one's faith. I saw one recently that promised biblical answers to "almost all your questions," including (according to the book's description) "Is body piercing wrong?" and "Can demons read our thoughts?"[74]

Again, I don't question the intentions of those who write or read these kinds of books, but I do think that their efforts are, in many cases, misguided. Moreover, the need for answers and certainty invariably leads to a posture of defensiveness that is ultimately rooted in fear—namely, the fear of being wrong and having to change our beliefs. In fact, we are so resistant to change that, as William H. Baker puts it, "we would often rather be wrong than change our minds."[75] Perspectives that differ from our own create an uncomfortable sense of cognitive dissonance, and we instinctively react to minimize the discomfort and the intellectual demands that it brings about. Adding a dose of authoritarianism to this already destructive response is a recipe for disaster. Taylor describes the result as follows:

---

[74] Towns, E. L. (2012). *Bible answers for almost all your questions.* Nashville, TN: Thomas Nelson.

[75] Baker, W. H. (1980). Defensiveness in communication: Its causes, effects, and cures. *Journal of Business Communication, 17*(3), 33–43.

> In environments tainted with authoritarianism, every question creates a mini-crisis. It raises, even if only momentarily, the possibility that the belief system is flawed or incomplete. ... For this reason, real questions are generally discouraged. Phony questions, however, where the answer is known by all, are part of a pleasurable ritual.[76]

Let's suppose for a moment that God didn't need us to defend Him, that He wasn't threatened by our questions, and that His plans were not dependent on our human understanding. In other words, let's suppose for a moment that God was... well, God.

Would we then be more willing to admit that we don't have it all figured out?

Would we be able to see that our attempts to defend God are really less about Him and more about us?

Would we be willing to say, unapologetically and without fear, "I don't know"? Or, "That's a good question"?

We need to say these words. And we need to say them often, not just for the sake of honesty, but also for the sake of living at peace with those who differ from us.

Baker suggests that

---

[76] Ibid., p. 36.

nondefensive, nonthreatening relationships with others can best be achieved by (a) empathizing or understanding *with* them as opposed to judging or evaluating them and their comments; (b) treating them as equals, as important and competent persons, as opposed to degrading them and their contributions; and (c) being congruent or genuine in every way. [77]

At the risk of discounting the value of Baker's work, let me simply say that these conclusions are not terribly surprising.

If we deny the reality of our own limitations, if we refuse to admit that there are things we don't know, then we should not be surprised when others perceive us to be disingenuous, insincere, or even delusional.

If our first impulse is to discredit, discount, or discard those who raise uncomfortable questions, then we should not be surprised when our relationships remain shallow, guarded, or nonexistent.

Social psychologist Morton Deutsch is widely known for his "crude law of social relations," which states that the effects elicited by a given type of social relationship also induce that type of relationship. So cooperation elicits cooperation, competition elicits competition, and—in the

---

[77] Ibid., p. 40.

context of our current discussion—defensiveness elicits defensiveness.[78]

If we wish to experience depth and openness in our relationships with diverse others, then we must resist the subconscious drive toward defensiveness and be willing to say, "I don't know."

We must also make the conscious choice to practice inquiry, empathy, and complexity.

We must say things like:

"Tell me more."

"What was that like?"

"Help me understand."

"I've never thought about it that way."

To the spiritually insecure, these words are dangerous. After all, the more I understand someone, the more difficult it becomes to pigeonhole them into a neat and tidy category—to write them off as a "them." If I allow myself to venture into the realm of another's lived experiences, then I may suffer the unpleasant and

---

[78] Deutsch, M. (2006). Cooperation and competition. In M. Deutsch, P. T. Coleman, & E. Marcus (Eds.), *The handbook of conflict resolution: Theory and practice* (2nd ed., pp. 23-42). San Francisco, CA: Jossey-Bass.

inconvenient side effect of empathy. I may even find that I have more in common with the "other" than I originally thought. In the worst case, I may find myself re-thinking my own positions or finding merit in a perspective that differs from my own—a devastating outcome for one whose faith requires unchallenged certainty.

Of course, the alternative to spiritual insecurity is not spiritual arrogance. Rather, it is spiritual humility—that is, to recall our earlier definition, a proper view of oneself in relation to God and others.

What are the habits of spiritual humility? I'll suggest four:

1. *Intellectual honesty*—in particular, an acceptance of the limitations of human reason and the impossibility of attaining a complete and consistent understanding of the divine.

2. *Curiosity*, because faith—and our understanding of God—is made stronger by diverse perspectives.

3. *Openness*. While the spiritually insecure are resistant to change, the way of humility calls us to be tentative in our beliefs and to value the pursuit of truth above our own correctness.

And last, but certainly not least:

4. *Confidence*—not in ourselves, but in a sovereign God whose plans will not be thwarted by humanity's failures, weaknesses, and sin.

What does it look like to bear witness to *this* God instead of the false god of fear and control? And how is spiritual humility compatible with Jesus' command to "make disciples of all nations"?[79] If humility and conviction can coexist, how does one live out a faith that balances the two? We'll consider these questions in the next chapter.

---

[79] Matthew 28:19

Chapter 6

Conviction

I work at a public university, and from time to time, street preachers visit our campus, ostensibly to share the gospel with the lost souls that populate our halls and our classrooms. Their version of sharing the gospel involves picket signs, tracts, yelling, and an ample dose of fear.

One day, not too long ago, I was walking with a friend and colleague who happens to attend the same church that I do. The street preachers had staked out a well-traveled pathway near our student union and were doing their usual thing.

We walked by, were offered a tract, politely said "no thank you," and kept on walking. That's when we heard, from behind us, a question that stopped us in our tracks: "Are you being intolerant?"

I think that both of us initially took the question to be a joke—that is, until it became painfully clear that it wasn't. My colleague's initial reaction was to ask, "Are you being serious?" When the street preacher responded in the affirmative (we were being intolerant for not taking his tract), the first thing that came to my mind was Inigo Montoya's famous quote from *The Princess Bride*: "You keep using that word. I do not think it means what you think it means."

The conversation that ensued was as unsettling as it was predictable.

We needed our sins forgiven. We were going to have to stand before God someday. Don't say that he (the street preacher) didn't warn us when we ended up in hell.

What made this conversation so disturbing was not so much its content—indeed, we are all sinners in need of forgiveness, and we will all be accountable to our Creator someday—but rather the context in which it took place. It was a one-sided message of fear and condemnation, delivered by a stranger, to a stranger, completely outside the bounds of any kind of mutual relationship or bond of trust.

There is a question that I always want to ask when I come across folks like this. The question is: What are you trying to accomplish? I assume that for most evangelists, the answer would be to save souls (or, for those who like to keep score, to *win* souls) by bringing them to Christ.

Which raises another question: Is it working? Based on my interactions with college students over the past 15 years, I would be shocked if this kind of judgmental, fear-based approach did anything other than alienate those who most need to hear the message of Christ. Worse yet, it perpetuates the negative stereotypes that keep many thoughtful and spiritually-sensitive young people from wanting to have anything to do with Christianity.

Does evangelism that begins with condemnation further the kingdom of God? Is it a victory for the kingdom to gain a follower of Christ who is motivated entirely by fear and has no concept of God's love and grace? Or would Jesus offer the same admonition to many modern-day evangelists as he did to the Pharisees in his time?

> Woe to you, teachers of the law and Pharisees, you hypocrites! You shut the door of the kingdom of heaven in people's faces. You yourselves do not enter, nor will you let those enter who are trying to.
>
> Woe to you, teachers of the law and Pharisees, you hypocrites! You travel over land and sea to win a single convert, and when you have succeeded, you make them twice as much a child of hell as you are. [80]

If I did not believe that humility and conviction were compatible, and indeed necessary complements of each other, then this book would be nothing more than an exercise in hypocrisy. At the same time, it seems to me that Jesus was and is concerned not only about the

---

[80] Matthew 23:13, 15

substance of our convictions, but also the way we express them.

The author of the book of James hammers this point home, drawing a stark contrast between earthly wisdom and the wisdom of God:

> Who is wise and understanding among you? Let them show it by their good life, by deeds done in the humility that comes from wisdom. But if you harbor bitter envy and selfish ambition in your hearts, do not boast about it or deny the truth. Such "wisdom" does not come down from heaven but is earthly, unspiritual, demonic. For where you have envy and selfish ambition, there you find disorder and every evil practice.
>
> But the wisdom that comes from heaven is first of all pure; then peace-loving, considerate, submissive, full of mercy and good fruit, impartial and sincere. Peacemakers who sow in peace reap a harvest of righteousness. [81]

Other translations describe heavenly wisdom as gentle, yielding to others, treating others with honor and dignity, not two-faced, and willing to yield to reason. Are these the kinds of attributes that are typically associated with Christians and Christianity, particularly in the context of evangelism? Sadly, I think not.

---

[81] James 3:13-18

One of my biggest concerns about modern-day evangelism is that it presents a version of the gospel that is not only rooted in fear, but also profoundly egocentric.

You are a sinner in danger of the fires of hell.

You need to be saved.

Jesus died for *you*.

In other words, it's all about *you*.

It's not that these things are necessarily untrue. But isn't the gospel of Jesus Christ bigger than this? Isn't God's redemptive plan about more than my narcissistic need to know that *I* am saved and that *I* will not have to endure the punishment that awaits those other less enlightened sinners?

The truth is so much more compelling and expansive than this.

We live a world that is both beautiful and broken.

We *all* have failed in ways big and small. Or, as Paul writes in Romans, "all have sinned and fall short of the glory of God." [82]

---

[82] Romans 3:23

The God who created us is the same God who redeems us—a God who *literally* brings life from death.

Jesus Christ, the God-man who conquered death, reigns from His throne of grace, boldly proclaiming, "I am making everything new!" [83]

All that is broken will one day be restored. All that is wrong will one day be made right. "He will wipe every tear from their eyes. There will be no more death or mourning or crying or pain, for the old order of things has passed away." [84]

This, my friends, is the good news of Jesus Christ, and it is so much more than a "get out of hell free" card.

In our zeal to win souls, we too often view conversion as the end goal, presenting faith as nothing more than intellectual assent to a set of beliefs or doctrines. In doing so, we lose sight of who we are and who God created us to be. In the book of Ephesians, Paul writes that "we are God's handiwork, created in Christ Jesus to do good works, which God prepared in advance for us to do." [85] The author of the book of James writes:

> Religion that God our Father accepts as pure and faultless is this: to look after orphans and widows in their

---

[83] Revelation 21:5
[84] Revelation 21:4
[85] Ephesians 2:10

distress and to keep oneself from being polluted by the world.... What good is it, my brothers and sisters, if someone claims to have faith but has no deeds? [86]

True faith is not just an exercise of the mind. Indeed, it should be nothing less than transformational. And yet, as Kinnaman and Lyons observe:

> Most people in America, when they are exposed to the Christian faith, are not being transformed. They take one step into the door, and the journey ends. ... The depth and texture of Christianity ought to appeal to young people, but the unChristian notion strains life in Christ into mere mental allegiance to a religion. [87]

I certainly don't mean to suggest that beliefs are not important. But I am concerned about the all-too-common tendency within Christianity to exalt ortho*doxy* (right beliefs) at the expense of ortho*praxy* (right practices). It would be one thing if this unhealthy focus on doctrine was limited to a few core tenets of the Christian faith, but the truth is that in many Christian circles, questioning the status quo—particularly on moral, social, or political issues—is enough to bring forth charges of heresy, and sometimes worse.

---

[86] James 1:27, 2:14

[87] Kinnaman, D., & Lyons, G. (2007). *Unchristian: What a new generation really thinks about Christianity... and why it matters.* Grand Rapids, MI: Baker Books. (p. 82)

I'm not talking here about people who question things like the divinity of Christ or the doctrine of the Trinity.

I'm talking about people like Ed Dobson whose allegiance to Christ was called into question because he voted for a Democrat.

Or Dan Haseltine, the lead singer of the band Jars of Clay, who made the mistake of using Twitter to pose questions—not rhetorical questions, but genuine questions to which he was seeking answers—about conservative arguments against same-sex marriage. The resulting uproar was merciless. Comments on social media included the following gems:

> Jars of Clay = lukewarm

> How could a person claim to follow and love Jesus and at the same time reject Jesus so much?

> It's amazing how people and pick and choose what they feel is 'seeking the truth in love' so Dans' stance in favor of homosexual marriage is 'truth' 'love'??? man, 60% of you people need to tie a boulder to your neck and do us all a favor. [88]

One of Haseltine's tweets that was apparently offensive enough to evoke suggestions of suicide was this:

---

[88] Corey, B. (2014, April 28). Shot for asking a question: What we can learn from the Jars of Clay fallout. Retrieved from http://www.patheos.com/blogs/formerlyfundie/jars-of-clay-fallout/

It is perhaps less important to know what is "right and wrong" morally speaking, than to know how to act toward those we consider "wrong."[89]

Does anyone else see the irony here?

The cultural conflation of theology and politics contributes to these kinds of disputes, but they are certainly not confined to the political realm.[90]

Just ask Rob Bell, who was (as you may recall from our earlier discussion) ostracized for expressing the *hope* and *possibility* that all of humanity would one day be reconciled to God.

Farewell Rob Bell? Blogger Tylor Standley suggests that if we are to be consistent, then "heretics" like C.S. Lewis, Martin Luther, St. Augustine, William Barclay, John Stott,

---

[89] https://twitter.com/scribblepotemus/status/458642193402826753

[90] The examples I've given here involve two Christians who have expressed or have been associated with politically or socially liberal positions. I'm not trying to suggest that conservatives have a monopoly on exclusionary behavior, but I also don't know of any examples of well-known Christians whose *faith* has been publicly questioned for supporting conservative causes. This may be simply a consequence of the fact that conservative positions are still largely the status quo within the American church. With that said, Christians who express or support conservative positions on issues like same-sex marriage often find themselves attacked and ostracized in other ways. The resignation of Mozilla's CEO and co-founder Brendan Eich, along with the 2012 boycotts of Chick-Fil-A, are good examples of how one's personal *beliefs*—apart from their actions toward others—can elicit strong condemnation from the communities and organizations to which they belong.

and Billy Graham should also be banned from evangelical Christianity.[91]

Of all these heretics, I have to say that C.S. Lewis is my favorite, in large part because of the openness with which he held his beliefs. For example, in *Mere Christianity*, Lewis spends a few pages reflecting on God's timelessness as it relates to prayer, foreknowledge, and free will. He provides a number of insightful metaphors to help shed some light on this mystery, but my favorite part of the chapter is the last paragraph, where Lewis writes, in regards to one possible explanation:

> This idea has helped me a good deal. If it does not help you, leave it alone. It is a "Christian idea" in the sense that great and wise Christians have held it and there is nothing in it contrary to Christianity. But it is not in the Bible or any of the creeds. You can be a perfectly good Christian without accepting it or indeed without thinking of the matter at all.[92]

C.S. Lewis, and others like him, seemed to understand that not all theological matters carry equal weight, and that "proper" theology is not a prerequisite for genuine

---

[91] Standley, T. (2014, May 7). 6 "heretics" who should be banned from evangelicalism (or, a lesson in consistency). Retrieved from http://andygill.org/heretics-banned-evangelicalism/

[92] Lewis, C. S. (1996). *Mere Christianity*. New York, NY: Touchstone. (p. 149)

faith in Christ. Another quote from *Mere Christianity* sums it up beautifully:

> We are told that Christ was killed for us, that His death has washed out our sins, and that by dying He disabled death itself. That is the formula. That is Christianity. That is what has to be believed. Any theories we build up as to how Christ's death did all this are, in my view, quite secondary: mere plans or diagrams to be left alone if they do not help us, and, even if they do help us, not to be confused with the thing itself. [93]

When will we stop confusing our theories about God with God Himself?

When will we begin to recognize the difference between truth, opinion, and preference?

Jesus said to the religious elite, "You study the Scriptures diligently because you think that in them you have eternal life. These are the very Scriptures that testify about me, yet you refuse to come to me to have life." [94]

Is our obsession with orthodoxy preventing us from experiencing the abundant, eternal life that is offered through Jesus Christ?

---

[93] Ibid., p. 59.
[94] John 5:39-40

And what version of Jesus does the world see in our lives? Do they experience through us the greatest redemptive force the world has ever known, a love so beautiful and freeing that even our hardened, rebellious hearts cannot resist it? Or do we simply put a Jesus stamp on the same old legalistic nonsense that has driven honest, seeking souls away from God in droves?

Let me say it again: I am not claiming that beliefs don't matter. And I'm not a relativist either.

Beliefs matter.

There *is* absolute truth, and *it* matters.

Jesus said, "If you hold to my teaching, you are really my disciples. Then you will know the truth, and the truth will set you free." [95] But the truth that Jesus taught—and indeed embodied—was a truth based in love.

The greatest commandment that Jesus gave us was to love God wholeheartedly and to love our neighbors as ourselves. To the one who accepted this teaching, Jesus replied, "You are not far from the kingdom of God." [96]

Jesus said that his disciples would be known for their love for one another. [97] He prayed that His followers would "be

---

[95] John 8:31-32
[96] Mark 12:34
[97] John 12:35

brought to complete unity" so that "the world will know that you [the Father] sent me and have loved them even as you have loved me." [98]

Truth. Love. Freedom. This is a message that the world desperately needs to hear. But how can followers of Christ break through the noise of the street preachers, the self-appointed judges, and the modern-day Pharisees to bear witness to this life-giving gospel of love and grace?

As far as I know, I have never "won" a single soul for Christ. I've told my story, and I've hopefully planted some seeds. But I've never led anyone to pray the sinner's prayer, and I have no tangible or easily quantifiable measure of my impact on the kingdom of God.

This is probably for the best. After all, if I was keeping score, I'm sure that I'd somehow find a way to make it all about me.

I am very grateful that God has given me a story to tell and, from time to time, perspectives on life that resonate with those who hear them. Every now and then, He surprises me by letting me know that something I've said or done has made a difference in someone's life.

One of the biggest recent surprises came in response to a banquet talk I gave at a conference on inquiry-based

---

[98] John 17:23

learning in mathematics. When I was invited to speak at this conference, I was in the midst of writing my Master's thesis on religiosity, authoritarianism, and social identity. In my talk, I reflected on how inquiry-based learning—which engages learners in the discovery of new concepts through questions, problems, and activities—has a lot in common with a questing approach to faith. It didn't seem like too much of a stretch to suggest that engagement in inquiry-based learning may have some pro-social effects on students.

I never mentioned God or Jesus in my talk, but I did include this quote from Rob Bell:

> Some communities don't permit open, honest inquiry about the things that matter most. Lots of people have voiced a concern, expressed a doubt, or raised a question, only to be told by their family, church, friends, or tribe: "We don't discuss those things here." I believe the discussion itself is divine. [99]

A few months later, I received an e-mail from a woman who had attended the conference, thanking me for the impact that my talk had had on her spiritual life. She shared with me that, for the past 20 years, she had been an atheist who thought that religion had nothing to offer her. She went on to say that my talk had prompted her to

[99] Bell, R. (2011). *Love wins: A book about heaven, hell, and the fate of every person who ever lived.* New York, NY: Harper-Collins. (p. ix)

re-examine this stance, and that she now belonged to a wonderful faith community and was very happy that she had opened herself up to this possibility.

Wow! What an amazing story! What a victory for the kingdom of God, that He would use a talk at a math conference to draw one of his beloved daughters back to Him. I couldn't have made this happen if I had tried. And that's the point.

I am convinced that the most effective evangelism takes place not in churches or arenas or on soapboxes, but in classrooms, factories, and on barstools.

Jesus' ministry was relational. He invested in his disciples. He ate with them. He prayed with them. He engaged them in dialogue. And he did so with patience, compassion, and grace—even when they completely missed the point of all that he had taught them. If we claim to follow Christ, we must do the same.

God has given each of us a story to tell and an audience to tell it to. Evangelism doesn't have to be forced, manipulative, judgmental, or obnoxious. In fact, billboards, tracts, and picket signs often serve only to build fences around the kingdom of God. But the convictions of the humble flow from an understanding of God's love for His people and His longing for relationship with them. If our actions toward those outside of

Christianity are not rooted in this love, then we have missed the point.

When humanity ate from the tree of the knowledge of good and evil, we succumbed to the temptation to become gods unto ourselves. A lesser god may have thrown in the towel, but the one true God did not. I firmly believe that, since the day humanity fell, the Holy Spirit has been at work, relentlessly pursuing the estranged children of God and wooing them back to Him.

God invites us to participate in this work of redemption, and He uses us as vessels to share His love and grace with a broken world. But we can't go it alone. No human effort can ever take the place of the Holy Spirit. Our convictions accomplish nothing if they do not align with God's greater plan and purpose. And our convictions are worse than useless if they are not held with humility.

I have come to believe that Jesus Christ is who He said He was: the way, the truth, the life, God incarnate, and the savior of the world. But this belief, no matter how strongly I hold it, does not require me to summarily discount the perspectives of those who believe differently. I've learned a lot from interacting with folks of different faiths, including those who don't believe in God at all. In many cases, hearing their experiences has broadened my view of who God is and convicted me of failures in my own life and in the life of the body of Christ.

And so I believe that as much as I have to offer those outside of Christianity, they have something to offer me as well. I must acknowledge that my understanding of God is neither complete nor infallible. If humility and conviction are to coexist in my life, I must be willing to admit that I could be wrong.

Chapter 7

Grace

I could be wrong.

Let me say it again: I could be wrong. Wrong about my theology, wrong about my interpretation of scripture, wrong about my criticism of the church, wrong about my views on humility and pride—perhaps even wrong to have even written this book in the first place.

I could be wrong about nearly everything I believe, and that would be okay as long as I was right about one thing: that God's grace is sufficient to cover all of my wrongness, and that my standing in His eyes does not depend on me getting it right. For me, it all comes down to grace, and I'll put all of my eggs in that basket.

Please don't misunderstand me here. There are days when I don't believe in God's grace the way I say I do. There are times when I try to earn my way to Him, even though I know that it is an exercise in futility. There have been periods of my life in which I have messed up so badly, strayed so far from God, that the story simply seemed too good to be true. To this day, there are times when I believe in God's grace just so I can sleep at night. After all, if I'm wrong about that—if God's grace isn't as big as I think it is—then, to put it bluntly, I'm screwed.

So I choose to believe that God's grace is everything I need it to be. Is this naïve and self-serving? Perhaps. But given a choice between naivety and despair, I'll choose the former every time.

And let's face it: If I'm wrong about God's grace, then I'm not the only one who's in trouble. Without God's grace, heaven looks pretty empty and hell looks pretty full.

Of course, there are some who accept and even celebrate this possibility. They quote verses like Matthew 7:13-14: "Enter through the narrow gate. For wide is the gate and broad is the road that leads to destruction, and many enter through it. But small is the gate and narrow the road that leads to life, and only a few find it."

At first glance, the interpretation of these verses seems obvious (at least the way it has been taught to many of us): the wide gate is for nonbelievers or Christians in name only, and the narrow gate is for the "real" Christians. The former go to hell, and the latter go to heaven.

But let me ask you this: in today's Christian culture, what exactly is the broad road that leads to destruction? And what does it mean to go against the flow and to find that narrow road that leads to life?

In my view, the answer to this question is really not much different than it was in Jesus' time. My pastor friend, Doug Bishop, puts it this way:

> The wide path was safe. It was comfortable. There was security in submitting to the authority and teachings of the priests, the scribes, and the Pharisees. All of whom were highly educated and had devoted their lives to the Scriptures so that they could show the people how to remain on the wide path to God.
>
> But look what happened. A Jewish carpenter's son showed up and dismantled all of their logic, their teachings and their man-made laws, which were put in place to keep people in their place.
>
> Jesus took the narrow path, and endured the scorn from the wide path tour guides. He demonstrated that theirs is the way of enslavement, not freedom. Theirs is the way of destruction, not life. They had created a form of godliness which completely preys on the God-placed longing in every human heart for a deep, intimate relationship with the Father. They became the toll-takers standing at the wide gate, enriching themselves on the natural desire we all have to experience eternal freedom. The only other choice? That

creaky, dangerous-looking gate over there that looks like it could get me killed if I step through it. [100]

And that's the crux of it, isn't it? Grace requires us to put it all on the line. Grace demands that we relinquish any claim we have to our own lives or our eternal destinies, placing our very souls into the care and custody of the Almighty. With grace, there is no room to hedge our bets, no room to beg forgiveness for our failures while still claiming credit for our victories. To do so is to deceive oneself and rob God of the glory He rightly deserves.

In Ephesians, Paul writes:

> But because of his great love for us, God, who is rich in mercy, made us alive with Christ even when we were dead in transgressions—it is by grace you have been saved. And God raised us up with Christ and seated us with him in the heavenly realms in Christ Jesus, in order that in the coming ages he might show the incomparable riches of his grace, expressed in his kindness to us in Christ Jesus. For it is by grace you have been saved, through faith—and this is not from yourselves, it is the gift of God—not by works, so that no one can boast. [101]

God is rich in mercy. *God* made us alive with Christ. *God* put the riches of *His* love and grace on display through *His*

---

[100] Bishop, D. (2013, June 19). Narrow path // wide path. Retrieved from https://www.adabible.org/sabea/2013/06/narrow-path-wide-path/
[101] Ephesians 2:4-9

kindness to us. And it is *God* who gave us the very gift of faith. We deny the truth if we allow ourselves to believe that we can add even one iota to the redemptive work of Jesus Christ.

Throughout history, humanity has wrestled with the question of what we must do to be made right with our Creator. Whether we admit it or not, we know our brokenness. We know that we have failed to live up to our own standards, let alone those of a holy God. And deep in our souls, we feel that there must be something we can do to set the record straight, to balance the scales and regain God's favor. In short, we long for *salvation*, both now and in the life to come.

Countless believers have been taught that to attain this salvation, we must pray the right prayer, believe the right doctrine, attend the right church, and have the kind of faith that bears spiritual fruit.

And so we pray the prayer, we do our best to believe the right things, we attend church and bible studies and small groups, and we strive to be loving, joyful, peaceful, patient, kind, good, gentle, faithful, and self-controlled. [102]

But we fail. Time and time again, we fail. We lust. We lie. We gossip. We covet. We rage. We worship the idols of greed and materialism. We ignore the widow and orphan.

---

[102] Galatians 5:22-23

We harbor bitterness and resentment. We nurse addictions—not just to alcohol or drugs, but to love, sex, work, success, approval, and our own pride. We break our promises. We feel more irritation than love toward our children. We argue. We fight. We complain. We sow seeds of discord. And, worse yet, we condemn those who do the same.

All the while, we are told by self-appointed spiritual guides—often our friends, family members, or clergy—that the way to conquer these demons is to draw nearer to God, to pray more, to spend more time in scripture... and the list goes on. Every moral failure becomes a spiritual failure. And with every sin, every step off the straight and narrow, the Accuser whispers in our ear, "Do you really think that God would accept someone like you?" Or, "If you were *really* saved, this wouldn't keep happening."

And we buy the lies—hook, line, and sinker. And so we pray the prayer again, we confess our sins, we muster up some forced sense of remorse, and we convince ourselves that this time, things will be different. That is, until we fall again. Each failure deepens our sense of shame and inadequacy, but like Sisyphus, we keep striving, blind to the futility of our efforts.

It is only when this cycle of disappointment and despair leaves us utterly ruined—when we find ourselves bruised and battered with nothing to show for it—that we can finally hear the gentle voice of the risen Christ, beckoning us home.

It is a death of sorts, an inevitable surrender to the reality of our own helplessness. But from this death, Jesus speaks words of life: "Come to me, all you who are weary and burdened, and I will give you rest." [103]

Jesus extends this invitation when we are at our worst. God Himself does not wait until we have our act together to offer His grace. Instead, He calls to us when we are worn out, beat up, and exhausted from our failed attempts to earn our way to Him. Jesus wasn't joking when he preached, "Blessed are the poor in spirit, for theirs is the kingdom of heaven." [104]

Brennan Manning—a man who understood grace better than most—wrote that "the disciple living by grace has undergone a decisive conversion—*a turning from mistrust to trust*. The foremost characteristic of living by grace is trust in the redeeming work of Jesus Christ." [105]

We all must decide where or in whom we will place our trust. In many areas of our lives, there is room for halfhearted trust—that is, trust with a backup plan. But

---

[103] Matthew 11:28

[104] Matthew 5:3

[105] Manning, B. (2005). *The ragamuffin gospel.* Colorado Springs, CO: Multnomah Books. (p. 76)

when it comes to faith, grace takes this option off the table. Grace is an all or nothing proposition. If we are still clinging to the notion that our salvation depends in part on us, then we have yet to fully embrace the gospel of grace.

What must we do to be made right with God? The answer is simple: Nothing. Absolutely nothing. Through His life, death, and resurrection, Jesus Christ has done what we cannot. With three tragically beautiful words, our suffering savior proclaimed from the cross a decisive victory over sin and death. It is finished. Done. Accomplished. Complete.[106]

---

[106] I realize that this paragraph is a bit of a theological land mine, so let me say a few words to elaborate on my perspective here. I suspect that some may object to the fact that I have omitted from my discussion any kind of requirement to accept or respond to God's grace. The key question here is whether we must accept forgiveness in order to be forgiven. My inclination is to say no, but I realize that many others believe differently. I am drawn to the view that Christ's death on the cross enacted forgiveness for all and that, through Him, all of humanity is made right with God— whether we accept it or not. At the same time, I believe that how we respond to the reality of our forgiveness is vitally important, both for this life and the next. I think it is entirely possible that some forgiven souls remain outside the gates of heaven simply because they choose not to enter, in effect rejecting the benefit of forgiveness. This may be an issue of semantics, and I don't want theological nuances to detract from the broader point I am trying to make—namely, that God's grace is entirely sufficient to accomplish our salvation and that there is nothing we can do to earn our way to Him. Ironically, my experience is that those who place conditions on God's grace often spend a lot of time thinking about how to meet those conditions, obsessing about exactly what it means to accept Christ and whether they have accepted Him the right way or with enough

When we come to grips with our own inadequacy and allow ourselves to dwell in the sufficiency of grace, the inevitable result is a transformation of our view of God, ourselves, and the people around us. For this reason, there is perhaps no stronger antidote to the poison of spiritual pride than a life lived by grace.

Grace demands that we abandon our false confidence in human understanding, trading earthly wisdom for that of Christ, who, as Paul writes," has become for us wisdom from God—that is, our righteousness, holiness and redemption."[107]

By grace, we have been forgiven. So too must we learn to forgive, bearing with each other's faults in love.

In grace, there is both unity and diversity: one hope, one Spirit, one body—but a body with many parts, each of them indispensible.

By grace, there is no us, no them, no boasting, no pulling rank, no claiming superiority on account of our

---

sincerity. To me, this sounds a lot like salvation by works. Conversely, those who most fully accept God's gift of grace are often those who have grown tired of such mental gymnastics and have simply given up on their ability to be sincere enough or repentant enough or whatever else might be required as a sign of genuine faith. The deepest level of trust seems to be found among those who believe that trust itself is a consequence, rather than a precondition, of salvation. Paradoxically, it may be that the way to truly realize our salvation is to stop trying to attain it.

[107] Ephesians 2:8-9

enlightened beliefs or pious deeds. Grace is the great equalizer that demolishes the boundaries of ethnocentrism. In doing so, grace evokes what Jonathan Sacks calls a "profound crisis of identity" in which "the boundaries of self and other, friend and foe, must be redrawn."[108]

On the other side of this crisis is a treasure of incomparable worth: peace.

---

[108] Sacks, J. (2003). *The dignity of difference: How to avoid the clash of civilizations.* New York, NY: Continuum. (p. 50)

Chapter 8

Peace

One of the most tangible byproducts of spiritual humility is peace.

We use the word *peace* a lot, probably without giving too much thought to its meaning. Sometimes peace signifies an absence of conflict. Other times, peace refers to a calm, serene feeling. When we say things like, "All I want is some peace and quiet," we are often expressing a longing to escape from the demands and busyness of life. In this sense, peace connotes rest and renewal.

As we near the end of our journey together, I would like to take a few moments to reflect on a deeper kind of peace. The peace I would like to explore is the peace of God— that is, the peace that comes from knowing and trusting the God of grace. It is, as Paul writes, a peace that "transcends all understanding," a peace that promises to "guard [our] hearts and [our] minds in Christ Jesus."[109]

---

[109] Philippians 4:7

What exactly does this peace look like? Is it an absence of conflict, a feeling of tranquility, or perhaps an escape from the troubles of life? Sadly, many Christians have been led to believe that faith in Christ promises all of these rewards. But Jesus taught the opposite.

Speaking to his disciples, Jesus said, "In this world you will have trouble. But take heart! I have overcome the world."[110] The peace of God comes not from the promise of a life without struggles, but from the encouragement of knowing that, in the end, Jesus Christ is and will be victorious—and we with Him. The trials we face will not consume us. Even when all seems lost, there is hope. In short, the story ends well.

Until then, however, we live in the first part of the verse. Jesus promised us that we would face trouble in this life. So many of Jesus' promises are beautiful and life-giving. But there is nothing beautiful about this one.

A few years ago, my wife, Melissa, and I experienced the most horrific summer of our lives. For me, it all started with a phone call.

I knew as soon as I picked up the phone that something was terribly wrong. Melissa was frantic. She said that she and our daughter, Zoey—whom we had adopted from West Africa just six months earlier—had run into each

---

[110] John 16:33

other coming around a corner. Zoey had fallen backwards and hit her head. Now she was vomiting and drifting in and out of consciousness.

I left the class I was teaching, raced home, and arrived to find a scene that would be a nightmare to any parent. The deputy who had responded to the 911 call was attempting to stabilize Zoey. My wife was in tears, trying to hold herself together. A few minutes later, the paramedics arrived, and Zoey was rushed to the hospital as a priority 1 trauma with a police escort.

The next few hours were terrifying. We learned that Zoey had a brain bleed—a subdural hematoma to be exact. She was in critical condition. A neurosurgeon was on call. And all we could do was wait to see whether the bleed would resolve itself or get worse.

After a long night in the pediatric ICU, things seemed to be looking up. Zoey was doing well, the bleed was resolving, and there would be no need for surgery. We breathed a sigh of relief and thanked God that we had apparently dodged a bullet. But our joy was short-lived.

Later that morning, two detectives showed up in our room. We had been told that, as a matter of procedure, the hospital was required to notify Child Protective Services whenever a child was admitted with a serious head injury. But having the police involved indicated to us that this was anything but routine.

The detectives separated us. They interrogated Melissa for 90 minutes. I got off easy with only a 45-minute interview. The detective who interviewed me said things like, "We want to be able to prove that your wife is innocent," and "I don't see why this is so traumatic for you." I remember thinking, over and over again, "Oh my God. They think that we did this."

From there, the situation went from bad to worse. The ophthalmologists found retinal hemorrhages, a symptom that is often associated with child abuse. There were interviews with social workers, "sitters" in Zoey's hospital room 24 hours a day (presumably to make sure that we didn't bludgeon her when no one was looking), and a palpable sense of fear and uncertainty that was unlike anything we had ever experienced.

It's hard to describe exactly what the next few days were like. Words like *shock*, *disbelief*, and *disorientation* only scratch the surface of the emotions we felt. We had to force ourselves to eat. We were constantly on edge. We hardly slept.

I distinctly remember that when I was able to get some rest, I would wake up and experience—for a moment at best—that sense of relief that one feels when they are roused from a nightmare, only to realize that the horrors they were experiencing were not real. But this was no dream. This was real.

When Zoey was released from the hospital five days later, it was not to us, but to my parents and sister. In fact, for over a week, none of our children were allowed to come home. When they did, it was only with the condition that Melissa not be alone with them while the investigation was pending.

There are few more effective ways to break a mother's heart than to tell her that she cannot be trusted with her own children. When terms like *first-degree child abuse* and *termination of parental rights* get thrown into the mix, the grief is nearly unbearable.

This went on for more than two months.

For the better part of the summer, we woke up each day knowing that our family was in jeopardy. We contemplated the possibility of someone else raising our children. We hired a criminal defense attorney and thought about things like trials and plea bargains and prison terms—all the while knowing that we had done absolutely nothing wrong.

And then, one morning in August, the ordeal ended as quickly as it began. With a phone call and a meeting from our case worker, it was over. No charges were being filed. The case was being closed. The investigation found no evidence of any abuse or neglect. Just like that, it was done.

I wish I could say that, looking back, I can see some grand redemptive purpose for what we experienced that summer. But I can't. It was horrible, and I wish that it had never happened. So why do I mention it here, in a chapter on peace of all places?

Jesus said, "In this life you will have trouble." It is intriguing to me that there are no conditions placed on this promise, no "unless you stay on the straight and narrow" or "but Jesus-followers will have *less* trouble." Pain, suffering, and brokenness seem to be universal elements of the human experience. And yet we still search for explanations for the trials we face.

Jesus' own disciples were not exempt from this tendency. Upon seeing a man who had been blind from birth, they asked Jesus, "Rabbi, who sinned, this man or his parents, that he was born blind?" Jesus response was, "Neither this man nor his parents sinned, but this happened so that the works of God might be displayed in him." [111]

Jesus disciples' were wed to a works-based, cause and effect, action-reaction form of spirituality. This is an

---

[111] John 9:1-3

understandable mindset, especially considering that the Jewish scriptures—the Old Testament—are full of verses that would seem to support it. For example:

> The Lord's curse is on the house of the wicked, but he blesses the home of the righteous. [112]

> No harm overtakes the righteous, but the wicked have their fill of trouble. [113]

> For the Lord watches over the way of the righteous, but the way of the wicked leads to destruction. [114]

> The Lord is far from the wicked, but he hears the prayer of the righteous. [115]

The disciples' question—Who sinned, this man or his parents?—is perfectly reasonable when viewed in light of these teachings. But Jesus' answer turns the whole system upside-down, in effect saying, "It's not that simple."

Unfortunately, some evangelical leaders seem to have missed the memo on this one. Just days after the September 11 terrorist attacks, Jerry Falwell appeared on *The 700 Club*, suggesting that God "[allowed] the enemies of America to give us probably what we deserve" on account of "the abortionists, and the feminists, and the

---

[112] Proverbs 3:33
[113] Proverbs 12:21
[114] Psalm 1:6
[115] Proverbs 15:29

gays and the lesbians who are actively trying to make that an alternative lifestyle, the ACLU, People for the American Way, all of them who have tried to secularize America."[116]

In the wake of the 2012 shootings at Sandy Hook Elementary School, James Dobson opined that "we have turned our back on the scripture and on God almighty and I think he has allowed judgment to fall upon us," connecting the tragedy in Newtown—which left 20 children and six staff members dead—to atheism, abortion, and same-sex marriage.[117]

In response to the comments of Dobson and others, Pastor and theologian Greg Boyd wrote:

> It seems to have become a staple of American conservative Christianity to respond to tragedy—when people most need to be reminded of God's comforting and healing love—to grab a megaphone and accuse. [118]

Sadly, he's right.

---

[116] Goodstein, L. (2001, September 19). Falwell: Blame abortionists, feminists, gays. *The Guardian*. Retrieved from http://www.theguardian.com/world/2001/sep/19/september11.usa9

[117] Wehner, P. (2012, December 21). The callous theology of James Dobson. *Patheos*. Retrieved from http://www.patheos.com/blogs/philosophicalfragments/2012/12/21/callous-theology-of-james-dobson/

[118] Boyd, G. (2012, December 18). Finger-pointing and the impulse to judge. *ReKnew*. Retrieved from http://reknew.org/2012/12/finger-pointing-and-the-impulse-to-judge/

When Zoey was in the hospital and all hell was breaking loose, my wife and I used Facebook to share updates and prayer requests with our family and friends. Perhaps the most honest post I wrote all summer was this one:

> Trying so hard to wrap my mind around what's happening to us. It just doesn't make sense.

I am so grateful that those who replied said things like:

> Jon, we're so sorry to hear the devastating news – you and Melissa and your family are continually in our thoughts and prayers.

> We are all here for you guys... you never have to feel like this is something you have to handle alone.

> Stop looking for rationality... it just is right now.

There were no lectures on how we needed to trust God more, or how He was trying to teach us something, or why God allowed this to happen to our family. There were no diagnoses or prescriptions, no three-step plans to coerce God into intervening on our behalf—just love, empathy, and a ceaseless stream of prayers. During those awful few months, we experienced the body of Christ at her best, the way God intended her to be.

I learned that summer that there is a peace that comes not from escaping the storms of life, but from experiencing

God in the midst of the storm. I think I had known this before, but it became real to me then.

Psalm 23 is one of the most quoted passaged of scripture. The words of the psalm are comforting in many ways, but they are also brutally honest:

> The Lord is my shepherd, I lack nothing.
>   He makes me lie down in green pastures,
> he leads me beside quiet waters,
>   he refreshes my soul.
> He guides me along the right paths
>   for his name's sake.
> Even though I walk
>   through the darkest valley,
> I will fear no evil,
>   for you are with me;
> your rod and your staff,
>   they comfort me.
>
> You prepare a table before me
>   in the presence of my enemies.
> You anoint my head with oil;
>   my cup overflows.
> Surely your goodness and love will follow me
>   all the days of my life,
> and I will dwell in the house of the Lord
>   forever.

There are times when God lays us down in green pastures. There are times when He leads us beside quiet waters and refreshes our souls. And there are times when He ushers us straight into the valley of the shadow of death, armed only with the promise that He is there with us.

About a week after Zoey's accident—when we still didn't know if or when our kids would be allowed to come home—we found ourselves sharing a meal with Melissa's parents at one of our favorite restaurants. It was a rare reprieve from the stress of the situation, and it made one verse from Psalm 23 come to life for me in a new way. The verse was this:

> *You prepare a table before me in the presence of*
> *my enemies.*

At that time, it seemed like so much of the world was against us. The doctors, the nurses, the social workers, the investigators, the detectives—none of them seemed to believe us. We couldn't explain our daughter's symptoms—never mind the fact that she had spent the first two years of her life in a third-world country—and so, in their view, there must have been something we were hiding.

And yet, in the midst of this chaos, God prepared a table for us where we could experience a taste—and a taste was all it was—of his grace and peace.

In the aftermath of the investigation, we learned that a number of mistakes had been made, from the way medical evidence had been interpreted to highly questionable—if not illegal—actions by certain case workers. A local law firm was ready to file a civil rights suit on our behalf, and for a while, we seriously considered it. We told ourselves that maybe doing so would prevent other families from having to experience what we had gone through. In the end, though, we decided not to move forward with the suit.

Although it was less clear then, I'm confident now that we made the right decision. Over time, God has gently impressed on my heart some difficult realities that have softened my views toward the case workers and medical professionals who, at the time, seemed intent on destroying all that we held dear.

I have thought a lot about what it must be like to work with abused children every day and to see unimaginable atrocities committed by parents and caregivers. I have thought about how easy it would be to become cynical and how difficult it must be to confront parents who are as adamant about their innocence as we were, and yet who have abused their children nonetheless. I have also learned, from the times that I have had to confront students about academic dishonesty, that being the accuser is no easy task—even when the evidence is strong.

And so, if I am honest with myself, I must at least entertain the possibility that the individuals involved in my daughter's case were acting in good faith and were doing their best to handle a difficult and unusual situation.

Were there mistakes made? Absolutely.

Did those mistakes cause my family an enormous amount of grief? Without a doubt.

Would it have been wrong for us to have pursued a legal remedy? Perhaps not. But it would not have been the way of grace. And it would not have been the way of peace.

If we truly understand the gospel of grace, we must acknowledge the extent to which we have been on the receiving end of God's undeserved mercy. And we must be willing to extend that same mercy to those around us— even those who cause us great pain.

Jesus taught us to love our enemies. He taught us to forgive as we have been forgiven. These are hard teachings to accept, particularly when we live in a world that is not as clear-cut as we would like it to be.

The wicked sometimes prosper. The righteous sometimes fall. And even this dichotomy is too simplistic. As Solomon wrote in the book of Ecclesiastes, "there is no one on earth who is righteous, no one who does what is right and never sins."[119] The categories of righteous and wicked are far too narrow to capture the complexity of the human condition.

Life *will* bring us trouble, but the gospel of grace frees us from the cycle of blame that demands explanations and accountability whenever we experience the brokenness of the world around us.

What if the troubles we face are neither punishment for our past sins nor divine coercion to induce future obedience? What if there is not always someone to blame? What if the pain we experience in this life is part of a greater plan and purpose that we have yet to see?

The gospel of grace begs us to trust that the second half of the verse is as true as the first:

> In this world you will have trouble. *But take heart! I have overcome the world.*

The peace of God dwells in the heart that trusts fully in the redemptive work of Jesus Christ. It is found and known by those who rest in the grace of God and, in doing so, are empowered to live lives of grace.

---

[119] Ecclesiastes 7:20

Grace is the essence of humility, and peace is its dividend. The world desperately needs to experience this peace, and those who claim to follow Christ have a special responsibility to bring it to fruition.

And so it is in that spirit that I leave you with a benediction that is both a prayer and a plea:

Grace and peace be with you, now and always.

Amen.

Further Reading

If you've enjoyed this book and would like to dig deeper, here are some good places to start:

Rob Bell (2013). *What we talk about when we talk about God*. New York, NY: HarperOne.

Ed Dobson (2009). *The year of living like Jesus*. Grand Rapids, MI: Zondervan.

David Kinnaman & Gabe Lyons (2007). *Unchristian: What a new generation really thinks about Christianity… and why it matters*. Grand Rapids, MI: Baker Books.

Anne LaMott. (2012). *Help, thanks, wow: The three essential prayers*. New York, NY: Penguin Group.

C.S. Lewis. (1996). *Mere Christianity*. New York, NY: Touchstone.

James MacDonald (2005). *Gripped by the greatness of God*. Chicago, IL: Moody Publishers.

Brennan Manning. (2005). *The ragamuffin gospel*. Colorado Springs, CO: Multnomah Books.

Richard Mouw. (2010). *Uncommon decency: Christian civility in an uncivil world*. 2nd ed. Downers Grove, IL: InterVarsity Press.

Jonathan Sacks (2003). *The dignity of difference: How to avoid the clash of civilizations*. New York, NY: Continuum.

Christian Smith (2011). *The Bible made impossible: Why biblicism is not a truly evangelical reading of scripture.* Grand Rapids, MI: Brazos Press.

Daniel Taylor (1992). *The myth of certainty: The reflective Christian and the risk of commitment.* Downers Grove, IL: InterVarsity Press.

Acknowledgements

This book would not have been possible without the support and inspiration of friends, family, colleagues, mentors, and loved ones.

My parents, inlaws, and extended family have all helped to shape my faith and my views on life.

I am particularly grateful for Paulo Valenza, Doug Bishop, Rick Hopkins, and Josh Lambert—brothers in Christ who have played an immeasurable role in my spiritual journey.

I own an enormous debt of gratitude to Bob Stains, who first sparked my interest in dialogue and peacebuilding, and to Karen Bhangoo Randhawa, Mike White, and Doug Kindschi, who advised the Master's thesis research that ultimately led to this book.

I am blessed to work with many wonderful colleagues, but none has been a better friend, mentor, and confidant than Matt Boelkins.

I'm very fortunate to be a part of Mars Hill Bible Church. I have learned a great deal from Rob Bell, Shane Hipps, and Kent Dobson.

Finally, my life would be only a shadow of what it is now without my wife, Melissa. I am so very thankful for her constant love and support—even when I do crazy things like writing a book on humility.

Follow J.K. Hodge on the web and on Twitter:

jkhodge.com

@JK_Hodge